# 1989 Cumulative Supplement to

# NORTH CAROLINA

# CRIMES

*A Guidebook on the Elements of Crime*

## Robert L. Farb and Benjamin B. Sendor

INSTITUTE OF GOVERNMENT • The University of North Carolina at Chapel Hill

THE INSTITUTE OF GOVERNMENT of The University of North Carolina at Chapel Hill is devoted to teaching, research, and consultation in state and local government.

Since 1931 the Institute has conducted schools and short courses for city, county, and state officials. Through monographs, guidebooks, bulletins, and periodicals, the research findings of the Institute are made available to public officials throughout the state.

Each day that the General Assembly is in session, the Institute's *Daily Bulletin* reports on the Assembly's activities for members of the legislature and other state and local officials who need to follow the course of legislation.

Over the years the Institute has served as the research agency for numerous study commissions of the state and local governments.

John L. Sanders, DIRECTOR
William A. Campbell, ASSOCIATE DIRECTOR

FACULTY

© 1990
INSTITUTE OF GOVERNMENT
The University of North Carolina at Chapel Hill
∞ This paper meets the minimum requirements
of American National Standard for Information Sciences—Permanence
of Paper for Printed Library Materials, ANSI Z39.48–1984.
Printed in the United States of America
ISBN 1-56011-168-2

# Contents

# Introduction

This cumulative supplement incorporates changes made in state laws since the publication of *North Carolina Crimes, A Guidebook on the Elements of Crime* (Third edition, 1985), which will be referred to as the "book" in this supplement. It explains statutory revisions of offenses discussed in that book, appellate court cases that change or clarify the case law regarding those offenses, and significant new offenses related to offenses discussed in the book, and it corrects errors. The period covered by this supplement includes statutory changes made through the 1989 session of the North Carolina General Assembly and cases decided through December, 1989, as reported through volume 325 of the *North Carolina Reports* and volume 96 of the *North Carolina Court of Appeals Reports*. It is designed to supersede the 1985 Supplement, which may be discarded. Page numbers direct the reader to the location in the book of the subjects discussed.

Benjamin B. Sendor is a former Institute of Government faculty member who is now with the Office of the Appellate Defender, Raleigh, North Carolina.

# 1
# States of Mind

---

**"Knowingly,"** *p. 2*: North Carolina does not accept the doctrine, accepted in some jurisdictions, that knowledge includes "willful blindness" of a highly probable fact (that is, deliberate avoidance of knowledge) (324 N.C. 190).

# 2

# Bars and Defenses

---

## DEFENSES SHOWING LACK OF BLAMEWORTHINESS

**Duress,** *p. 10*: The defense of duress may not be successfully asserted when the offense continues to be committed after the duress has ended. For example, a defendant charged with impaired driving could not assert the defense that he was attempting to escape from a group of people chasing him on foot if that incident preceded the time of the offense by thirty minutes, since his assailants would have been left behind long before (94 N.C. App. 386).

**Entrapment,** *p. 11*: Although defendants may not raise the defense of entrapment if they deny committing the underlying acts of the alleged crime (302 N.C. 623), they may raise the defense if they deny having the intent to commit the offense (306 N.C. 566; 95 N.C. App. 56).

**Voluntary intoxication,** *p. 11*: Delete the last sentence in this section that states that North Carolina does not recognize the doctrine of diminished capacity (see discussion below).

**Diminished capacity** [new section to be added after **Voluntary intoxication**], *p. 11*: The North Carolina Supreme Court now accepts the defense of diminished capacity (at least as a defense to the element in first-degree murder that provides that the defendant formed the specific intent to kill after premeditation and deliberation). Under this defense, defendants whose mental conditions at the time of an alleged offense do not satisfy the criteria of the insanity defense can still introduce evidence of their conditions to negate a mental element of the offense by showing that their conditions prevented them from forming the state of mind required by that mental element (322 N.C. 243).

# 3
# Participants in Crimes

## PRINCIPALS—ACTING IN CONCERT

*Elements, p. 16*:

[The elements should read as follows.]

A person is a principal to a crime if that person:

(1) with the required state of mind

(2) (a) participates in at least one of the acts necessary to the commission of the crime, *or*

(b) is present when the offense is committed and the person's participation indicates a shared purpose with someone whose actions satisfy all elements of the offense, *and*

(3) one or more of the co-participants engages in the acts not engaged in by the person that constitute the remainder of the crime.

*Notes*

**In general,** *p. 16*: Delete the citation (24 N.C. App. 484) to the first sentence in this section. It is not necessary that a defendant do any particular act constituting at least part of a crime to be convicted of that crime under the acting-in-concert principle so long as the defendant is acting together with another who does the acts necessary to constitute the crime pursuant to a common plan or purpose to commit the crime (297 N.C. 349). A judge may instruct the jury on both theories—acting in concert and aiding and abetting—when the facts in a case support both theories (313 N.C. 80).

## AIDING AND ABETTING FELONY

*Notes*

**In general** [new note to be added after *Punishment*], *p. 17*: A judge may instruct the jury on both theories—acting in concert and aiding and abetting—when the facts in a case support both theories (313 N.C. 80).

**Element (1),** *p. 17*: A case citation in addition to 113 N.C. 716 in this note is 283 N.C. 261. When a principal pled guilty to voluntary manslaughter, the defendant as an aider and abettor was properly convicted at a later trial of second-degree murder (24 N.C. App. 717).

# ACCESSORY BEFORE THE FACT TO FELONY

*Notes*

**Element (1),** *p. 19*: The prosecution must prove that the defendant's conduct caused or directly contributed to the other person's commission of the felony (319 N.C. 620).

**Relationship to conspiracy** [new note to be added after **Guilt for crimes other than that counseled**], *p. 19*: Since an agreement to commit an offense required to prove conspiracy is not an element of accessory before the fact to a felony, a defendant may be convicted of both conspiracy and the offense for which the defendant participated as an accessory before the fact if the defendant's conduct satisfies the elements of both offenses (294 N.C. 1; 313 N.C. 132).

# 4

# General Crimes

## ATTEMPT

*Related offenses not in this chapter, p. 23*:

The last two items in the list, attempted rape and attempted sexual offense, are not common law offenses; they are set forth in G.S. 14-27.6.

## SOLICITATION OF ANOTHER TO COMMIT A FELONY

*Punishment, p. 24*:

Solicitation to commit common law robbery is infamous (317 N.C. 164). G.S. 14-18.1, enacted by Chapter 734 of the Session Laws of 1989, makes solicitation to commit murder a Class E felony punishable by a maximum imprisonment of thirty years (presumptive sentence nine years) and/or a fine. However, if the solicitation to commit murder is of a law enforcement officer, judge or justice, former judge or justice, prosecutor or former prosecutor, juror or former juror, or witness or former witness against the defendant while the person is engaged in performing official duties or because of the person's exercise of official duties, it is a Class D felony punishable by a maximum imprisonment of forty years (presumptive sentence twelve years) and/or a fine.

## CONSPIRACY

*Punishment, p. 24*:

G.S. 14-18.1, enacted by Chapter 734 of the Session Laws of 1989, makes conspiracy to commit murder a Class E felony punishable by a maximum imprisonment of thirty years (presumptive sentence nine years) and/or a fine. However, if the conspiracy to commit murder is of a law enforcement officer, judge or justice, former judge or justice, prosecutor or former prosecutor, juror or former juror, or witness or former witness against the defendant while the person is engaged in performing official duties or because of the person's exercise of official duties, it is a Class D felony punishable by a maximum imprisonment of forty years (presumptive sentence twelve years) and/or a fine.

*Notes*

**Element (2),** *p. 25*: A defendant who enters into one agreement to commit multiple offenses may be convicted of only one count of conspiracy (of course, the defendant may still be convicted of any offenses actually committed pursuant to the conspiracy). It is the number of separate agreements, not the number of offenses the conspirators agree to commit, that determines the number of conspiracy charges (313 N.C. 572; 84 N.C. App. 150).

**Guilt as principal,** *p. 25*: Since the agreement to commit an offense required to prove conspiracy is not an element of accessory before the fact to a felony, a defendant may be convicted of both conspiracy and the felony for which the defendant participated as an accessory before the fact if the defendant's conduct satisfies the elements of both offenses (294 N.C. 1; 313 N.C. 132).

# 5

# Homicide

## FIRST-DEGREE MURDER

*Elements, page 30:* The book incorrectly lists malice, element (3), as an element of first-degree murder committed by killing another living human being during the commission of a felony, which is reflected in element (4)(c). Malice is not an element of that kind of first-degree murder (292 N.C. 455; 315 N.C. 398). Also, it is unclear whether malice is an element of first-degree murder committed by killing another living human being by poisoning, lying in wait, imprisonment, starvation, or torture, which is reflected in element (4)(b) (320 N.C. 179; 317 N.C. 193; 315 N.C. 398; 305 N.C. 400). However, given the absence of a direct ruling by our appellate courts, it will be listed as an element. The elements should read as follows:

A person is guilty of this offense if that person:

(1) kills

(2) another living human being

(3) (a) (i) with malice and
    (ii) specific intent to kill formed after premeditation and deliberation; *or*
  (b) (i) with malice and
    (ii) by poisoning, lying in wait, imprisonment, starvation, or torture; *or*
  (c) while committing or attempting arson, rape, sex offense, robbery, kidnapping, burglary, or any felony in which a deadly weapon is used.

*Punishment, p. 30:* Chapter 693 of the Session Laws of 1987 eliminated the death penalty for first-degree murder for a defendant who is under age seventeen at the time of the murder, and it set life imprisonment as the mandatory sentence for such a defendant. The act retained the death penalty as a possible sentence if a defendant under age seventeen commits first-degree murder while serving a prison sentence for a prior murder or while on escape from a prison sentence for a prior murder.

*Notes* **Elements (1) and (2),** *p. 31* [listed above as (3)(a)(i) and (3)(b)(i)]: The North Carolina Supreme Court has reaffirmed the common law rule that it is not murder to kill a viable, unborn fetus; it is murder only if the fetus is born alive and later dies of injuries inflicted before birth (324 N.C. 87).

**Element (3),** *p. 31*: A jury may infer malice from the intentional infliction of a wound with a deadly weapon even in a case of an alleged mercy killing (321 N.C. 186). Malice can also be inferred from the use of hands alone to inflict a fatal injury when an adult assaults an infant (320 N.C. 51).

**Element 4(a),** *p. 31* [listed above as (3)(a)(ii)]: Circumstances showing premeditation and deliberation can also include statements made by a defendant before the victim's death that indicate ill will toward the victim (313 N.C. 132).

**Element 4(b),** *p. 31* [listed above as (3)(b)(ii)]: The North Carolina Supreme Court has clarified the elements required to prove murder from killing by poisoning, lying in wait, imprisonment, starvation, or torture. Specific intent to kill, premeditation, and deliberation are not elements of this category of murder. Consequently, those mental states need not be—and are not—presumed or inferred from a killing in this category. The sole elements of this category of murder are killing another living human being with malice through use of one of the five designated methods (320 N.C. 179; 319 N.C. 152; 317 N.C. 193).

**Element 4(c),** *p. 32* [listed above as (3)(c)]: Discharging a firearm into occupied property amounts to a felony in which a deadly weapon is used, thereby supporting a felony murder conviction if death results (316 N.C. 78). A felony was committed with the use of a deadly weapon when the defendant carried a gun while committing felonious larceny, even though he did not use it to commit the larceny (315 N.C. 191). The prosecution need not elect for submission to a jury between theories of felony murder and murder with specific intent formed after premeditation and deliberation if its proof satisfies the elements of both types of murder (313 N.C. 516).

**Lesser-included offenses** [new note to be added after **Proximate cause**], *p. 32*: Involuntary manslaughter is a lesser-included offense of first- and second-degree murder and voluntary manslaughter (314 N.C. 649).

---

# SECOND-DEGREE MURDER

*Notes*    **Generally,** *p. 32*: Chapter 694 of the 1989 Session Laws amended G.S. 14-17 to include within second-degree murder a murder proximately caused by the unlawful distribution of cocaine when the ingestion of that cocaine causes the user's death.

**Lesser-included offenses** [new note to be added after **Generally**], *p. 32*: Involuntary manslaughter is a lesser-included offense of first- and second-degree murder and voluntary manslaughter (314 N.C. 649).

---

# VOLUNTARY MANSLAUGHTER

*Notes*    **Element (3),** *p. 33*: The distress that prompts a person to commit a mercy killing to end an ill relative's extreme physical suffering does not constitute adequate provocation; thus, it does not negate malice, and a mercy killing is properly categorized as first-degree murder rather than voluntary manslaughter (321 N.C. 186).

---

# INVOLUNTARY MANSLAUGHTER

*Elements, p. 34*: [The elements should read as follows.]

A person is guilty of this offense if that person:

(1) kills

(2) another living human being

(3) unlawfully

  (a) by an unlawful act that does not amount to a predicate felony for felony murder or is not inherently dangerous to life; *or*

  (b) by engaging in any other conduct in such a reckless and careless manner as to show a thoughtless disregard for consequences or a heedless indifference to the rights and safety of others; *or*

  (c) by a culpable omission to perform a legal duty.

*Notes*  **Element (3)** [new note to be added after **Elements (1) and (2)**], *p. 35*: The North Carolina Supreme Court has ruled that the kinds of conduct described in Elements (3)(a), (3)(b), and (3)(c) as set out above are not actually elements of involuntary manslaughter. Rather, Element (3) is the unlawful status of a particular killing and Elements (3)(a), (3)(b), and (3)(c) are merely three alternative grounds on which the prosecution may base its allegation and proof of unlawfulness (314 N.C. 649).

**Element (3)(a),** *p. 35*: Proof that the defendant was committing the offense of impaired driving that proximately caused the victim's death is sufficient evidence of involuntary manslaughter; the state need not also prove that the defendant's impairment caused the defendant to violate some other rule of the road that caused the victim's death (314 N.C. 633).

**Lesser-included offenses** [new note to be added after **Element 3(c)**], *p. 35*: In a case in which a defendant's impaired driving renders a resulting killing unlawful, felony death by vehicle is not a lesser-included offense of involuntary manslaughter. In contrast, misdemeanor death by vehicle is a lesser-included offense of involuntary manslaughter (90 N.C. App. 614; 71 N.C. App. 581; 33 N.C. App. 633; 31 N.C. App. 93).

# DEATH BY VEHICLE—FELONY

*Notes*  **Generally,** *p. 36*: Felony death by vehicle is not a lesser-included offense of involuntary manslaughter (90 N.C. App. 614). Therefore, the statement in the book that it is a lesser-included offense is now incorrect.

# DEATH BY VEHICLE—MISDEMEANOR

**Lesser-included offenses** [new note to be added after **Element (5)**], *p. 37*: Misdemeanor death by vehicle is a lesser-included offense of involuntary manslaughter (90 N.C. App. 614; 71 N.C. App. 581; 33 N.C. App. 633; 31 N.C. App. 93).

# 6

# Assaults

## SIMPLE ASSAULT

*Notes*    **Battery,** *p. 42*: When a battery is committed, the state is not required to show that the victim was placed in fear (266 N.C. 103; 18 N.C. App. 208).

## ASSAULT WITH A DEADLY WEAPON

*Notes*    **Element (2),** *p. 43*: A pistol is a deadly weapon even if a defendant uses it only to strike rather than to shoot the victim (87 N.C. App. 626). The use of hands or feet to inflict injury on an infant or disabled person may permit a finding that they were used as deadly weapons (309 N.C. 512). The use of fire to burn a house and harm a person inside supports a finding that the fire was a deadly weapon (315 N.C. 749).

## ASSAULT ON LAW ENFORCEMENT OR CUSTODIAL OFFICER

*Elements, p. 45:*    [The elements should read as follows.]
A person is guilty of this offense if that person:
(1) commits an assault
(2) on someone the person knows to be a law enforcement officer, a custodial officer of the State Department of Correction, an official of a detention facility, or an official of a juvenile training school
(3) who is discharging or attempting to discharge a duty of that office.

*Notes*    **Element (2),** *p. 46*: The statement that company police are not "law enforcement officers" covered by this statute is probably incorrect. Neither this statute nor G.S. 14-34.2 defines "law enforcement officer," but another statute and certain court decisions suggest that company police officers are covered by the term in some circumstances. Since G.S. 74A-2 authorizes company police officers to make arrests on specified types of property, they appear to fit the definition of law enforcement officer under G.S. 14-288.1(5), which includes any "person authorized under the laws of North Carolina to make arrests and . . . acting within his territorial jurisdiction." Also, the court of appeals has characterized company police officers as "public, although limited police officer[s]" in contrasting them with private detectives (17 N.C. App. 701). One possible qualification in their status is that they might be law enforcement officers when enforcing state law, but not when acting solely to protect private interests of their employers (205 N.C. 51). In circumstances in which company police officers both enforce state law and protect their employer's private interests, they would be law enforcement officers.

The second paragraph of this note in the book states, "It would seem that . . . the defendant must know that the person whom he assaults is a law enforcement officer." The North Carolina Supreme Court has since ruled that the state must prove that the defendant knew the person he or she assaulted was a law enforcement officer (315 N.C. 1).

To be covered by this statute, the duty performed by an officer need not be a duty required by law. For example, a law enforcement officer investigating a minor traffic accident that the officer has no duty to investigate is still discharging a duty of his or her office (88 N.C. App. 139).

# ASSAULT ON SCHOOL TEACHER OR ADMINISTRATOR

*Elements, p. 47*:  [The elements should read as follows.]
A person is guilty of this offense if that person:
(1) commits an assault
(2) on someone the person knows to be a schoolteacher, substitute teacher, teacher's aide, or administrator
(3) who is discharging or attempting to discharge an official duty.

# ASSAULT ON SOCIAL SERVICES EMPLOYEE

[This is a new offense to be inserted after **ASSAULT ON SCHOOL TEACHER OR ADMINISTRATOR,** *p. 47.*]

*Statute*  [Discussed below is only subsection (b)(7) of G.S. 14-33, which was enacted by Chapter 321 of the Session Laws of 1985 (not reproduced in this supplement).]

*Elements*  A person is guilty of this offense if the person:
(1) commits an assault

(2) on someone the person knows to be the director of the county department of social services, an administrator or other person in a supervisory position, social worker, eligibility specialist, or receptionist

(3) who is discharging or attempting to discharge a duty of that office or employment.

*Punishment*    Misdemeanor punishable by maximum imprisonment of two years and/or a fine.

*Notes*    **Element (1).** See the notes on forms of assault and battery under SIMPLE ASSAULT in the book on page 41.

**Elements (2) and (3).** This offense is similar to ASSAULT ON LAW ENFORCEMENT OR CUSTODIAL OFFICER in its application to people in specified occupations while they are discharging their duties. See the notes on element (2) under that offense in the book on page 46.

# DISCHARGING BARRELED WEAPON OR FIREARM INTO OCCUPIED PROPERTY

*Notes*    **Element (2),** *p. 55*: A firearm is discharged "into" occupied property even if the firearm is located inside the property, as long as the defendant is not inside the property. For example, a person commits this offense when standing outside a car and holding and firing a pistol through the car window even though the pistol is inside the car when it is fired (321 N.C. 464; 321 N.C. 663).

**Convictions permitted for both assault with a deadly weapon and discharging a barreled weapon or firearm into occupied property** [new note to be inserted after **Felony Murder**)], *p. 56*: A person may be charged and convicted of both discharging a barreled weapon or firearm into occupied property and assault with a deadly weapon (88 N.C. App. 428).

# ASSAULT WITH FIREARM OR OTHER DEADLY WEAPON ON LAW ENFORCEMENT OFFICER OR FIREMAN OR EMERGENCY MEDICAL SERVICES PERSONNEL

*Notes*    **Element 3,** *p. 57*: An additional citation for this note is 315 N.C. 1.

**Element 3(a),** *p. 57*: See this supplement's discussion in ASSAULT ON LAW ENFORCE-MENT OR CUSTODIAL OFFICER concerning when a company police officer may probably be considered a law enforcement officer under this statute.

**Element (4),** *p. 57*: To be covered by this statute, the duty performed by the officer, firefighter, or medic need not be a duty required by law. For example, a law enforcement officer investigating a minor traffic accident that the officer has no duty to investigate is still discharging a duty of his or her office (88 N.C. App. 139).

# CHILD ABUSE (MISDEMEANOR)

*Notes*  **Predicate for manslaughter,** *p. 60*: The correct case citation is 295 N.C. 559.

**Child abuse reporting,** *p. 61*: Although G.S. 7A-543 does not impose a criminal penalty for failing to report child abuse, a common law rule provides that if a statute either prohibits an act or commands the performance of an act, and the statute does not impose a sanction for violations, then a violation of the act is a general misdemeanor, punishable by maximum imprisonment of two years and/or a fine (228 N.C. 371; 94 N.C. 918; 75 N.C. 15).

# CHILD ABUSE INFLICTING SERIOUS INJURY (FELONY), *p. 61*:

[Substitute the following elements and notes for those in the book, due to revisions made by Chapter 668 of the Session Laws of 1985.]

*Statute*  **§ 14-318.4. Child abuse a felony.**

(a) A parent or any other person providing care to or supervision of a child less than 16 years of age who intentionally inflicts any serious physical injury upon or to the child or who intentionally commits an assault upon the child which results in any serious physical injury to the child is guilty of a Class H felony.

(a1) Any parent of a child less than 16 years of age, or any other person providing care to or supervision of the child, who commits, permits, or encourages any act of prostitution with or by the juvenile is guilty of child abuse and shall be punished as a Class H felon.

(a2) Any parent or legal guardian of a child less than 16 years of age who commits or allows the commission of any sexual act upon a juvenile is guilty of a Class H felony.

(b) The felony of child abuse is an offense additional to other civil and criminal provisions and is not intended to repeal or preclude any other sanctions or remedies.

*Elements*  A person is guilty of this offense if that person:
(1) (a) being a parent of a child less than sixteen years of age, *or*
    (b) being a person providing care or supervision to a child less than sixteen years of age
(2) (a) intentionally inflicts on or to the child, *or*
    (b) intentionally commits an assault on the child which results in
(3) serious physical injury.

*Punishment*  Class H felony punishable by maximum imprisonment of ten years and/or fine (presumptive three years).

*Notes*     **Elements (2)(a) and (2)(b).** The state must prove only that the defendant intentionally inflicted injury that proved to be serious; the state need not prove that the defendant intended to inflict serious injury (316 N.C. 168, a case decided under the former version of the statute but equally applicable to the revised version).

**Element (3).** See page 43 (Element (2) of ASSAULT INFLICTING SERIOUS INJURY) of the book for a discussion of what constitutes serious injury.

**Child-abuse reporting.** G.S. 7A-543 requires any person or institution that suspects that a child has been abused to report the incident to the director of the county social services department, but it does not impose a criminal penalty for failure to do so. However, a common law rule provides that if a statute either prohibits an act or commands the performance of an act, and the statute does not impose a sanction for a violation, then a violation of the act is a general misdemeanor, punishable by maximum imprisonment of two years and/or a fine (228 N.C. 371; 94 N.C. 918; 75 N.C. 15).

# CHILD ABUSE—PROSTITUTION (FELONY)

*Punishment, p. 62*:     Chapter 509 of the Session Laws of 1985 changed the offense to a Class H felony punishable by maximum imprisonment of ten years and/or a fine (presumptive sentence three years).

# CHILD ABUSE—SEXUAL ACT (FELONY)

*Punishment, p. 63*:     Chapter 509 of the Session Laws of 1985 changed the offense to a Class H felony punishable by maximum imprisonment of ten years and/or a fine (presumptive sentence three years).

# CONTRIBUTING TO A JUVENILE'S BEING DELINQUENT, UNDISCIPLINED, ABUSED, OR NEGLECTED

*Notes*     **Element (6)(c),** *p. 64*: Chapter 695 of the Session Laws of 1987 expanded the definition of an abused juvenile in G.S. 7A-517(1)(c). It provides that a child is abused if its parent or other person responsible for its care commits, permits, or encourages the commission of any of the following acts with or on the child: first- or second-degree rape or sexual offense; sexual act by custodian; crime against nature; incest; indecent liberties as provided in G.S. 14-202.1 (regardless of the ages of the parties); and offenses involving obscenity, sexual exploitation, and prostitution in G.S. 14-190.5 through 14-190.8 and 14-190.14 through 14-190.18.

# HARASSING PHONE CALLS

*Notes*   **Calls made or received by machines** [new note to be added after **Entrapment**], *p. 73*: Chapter 305 of the Session Laws  amended G.S. 14-196 to make clear that the statute's prohibitions also applied to telephonic communications made or received by a telephone answering machine or recorder, telefacsimile machine, or computer modem.

# 7

# Sexual Assault

## FIRST-DEGREE FORCIBLE RAPE

*Elements, p. 76:*  (2)(b) This element should read: "the defendant's legal spouse if they are living apart."

Chapter 742 of the Session Laws of 1987 deleted the requirement that spouses must be living apart "pursuant to a written agreement or judicial decree." Thus, a spouse may be prosecuted simply if both spouses are living apart when the offense is committed.

*Notes*  **Element (1),** *p. 77:* Proof of an erection is not required to establish penetration (314 N.C. 337).

**Element (2),** *p. 77:* Chapter 742 of the Session Laws of 1987 deleted the requirement that spouses must be living apart pursuant to "a written agreement or judicial decree." Thus, a spouse may be prosecuted simply if both spouses are living apart when the offense is committed.

**Element (3),** *p. 77:* The force does not include the conduct that constitutes the sexual act itself (72 N.C. App. 300). A child's general fear of a parent's authority over the child can constitute force (319 N.C. 34).

**Element 5(b),** *p. 78:* The injury can even be inflicted after the sexual act if it is so related to the sexual act that the infliction of injury and the sexual act form a continuous transaction (314 N.C. 232).

**Lesser-included offenses** [new note to be added after **Attempts**], *p. 78:* Assault on a female is not a lesser-included offense of rape or attempted first- and second-degree forcible rape (322 N.C. 733; 318 N.C. 669).

**Punishment for separate acts,** *p. 78:* Each separate act of sexual intercourse that constitutes rape is a separate, punishable offense (319 N.C. 656; 87 N.C. App. 199, *affirmed*, 322 N.C. 108; 31 N.C. App. 556).

## SECOND-DEGREE FORCIBLE RAPE

*Elements, p. 79:*  (2)(b) This element should read: "the defendant's legal spouse if they are living apart."

Chapter 742 of the Session Laws of 1987 deleted the requirement that spouses must be living apart "pursuant to a written agreement or judicial decree." Thus, a spouse may be prosecuted simply if both spouses are living apart when the offense is committed.

*Notes*      **Element (3)(a),** *p. 80*: Nonconsensual intercourse with a sleeping victim can be forcible (320 N.C. 387). The force does not include the conduct that constitutes the sexual act itself (72 N.C. App. 300). A child's general fear of a parent's authority over the child can constitute constructive force (319 N.C. 34).

**Element (3)(b),** *p. 80*: A sleeping victim is "physically helpless" under this statute (320 N.C. 387).

# FIRST-DEGREE FORCIBLE SEXUAL OFFENSE

*Elements, p. 82*:      (2)(b) This element should read: "the defendant's legal spouse if they are living apart."

Chapter 742 of the Session Laws of 1987 deleted the requirement that spouses must be living apart "pursuant to a written agreement or judicial decree." Thus, a spouse may be prosecuted simply if both spouses are living apart when the offense is committed.

*Notes*      **Element (1),** *p. 83*: Although proof of penetration is not required to prove cunnilingus or analingus, it is required to prove anal intercourse (316 N.C. 714).

**Element (2),** *p. 83*: Chapter 742 of the Session Laws of 1987 no longer requires that spouses must be living apart "pursuant to a written agreement or judicial decree." Thus, a spouse may be prosecuted simply if both spouses are living apart when the offense is committed.

**Element (3),** *p. 83*: The force does not include the conduct that constitutes the sexual act itself (72 N.C. App. 300). A child's general fear of a parent's authority over the child can constitute constructive force (319 N.C. 34).

**Element 5(b),** *p. 84*: The injury can even be inflicted after the sexual act if it is so related to the sexual act that the infliction of injury and the sexual act form a continuous transaction (314 N.C. 232).

# SECOND-DEGREE FORCIBLE SEXUAL OFFENSE

*Elements, p. 86*:      [The elements should read as follows.]
A person is guilty of this offense if that person:
(1) engages in a sexual act other than vaginal intercourse
(2) with
    (a) someone other than the person's legal spouse *or*
    (b) the person's spouse if they are living apart

(3) and the act is
    (a) by force and against the victim's will *or*
    (b) with someone who is
        (i) mentally defective *or*
        (ii) mentally incapacitated *or*
        (iii) physically helpless which is or should be known by the person.

*Notes*    **Element 3(a),** *p. 86*: A nonconsensual sexual act with a sleeping victim can be forcible (320 N.C. 387). The force does not include the conduct that constitutes the sexual act itself (72 N.C. App. 300). A child's general fear of a parent's authority over the child can constitute constructive force (319 N.C. 34).

        **Element 3(b),** *p. 86*: A sleeping victim is "physically helpless" (320 N.C. 387).

# FIRST-DEGREE STATUTORY SEXUAL OFFENSE

*Statute, p. 87*:    This offense is set forth in subsection (a)(1) of G.S. 14-27.4, not subsection (a)(2) as stated in the book.

# SEXUAL ACTIVITY BY A CUSTODIAN

*Notes*    **Element (1),** *p. 90*: Whether a patient is voluntarily or involuntarily committed to a hospital, he or she is still considered to be in the hospital's custody; a nurse was properly convicted of this offense when he had sexual intercourse with a patient who was voluntarily in a hospital (319 N.C. 358).

# INDECENT LIBERTIES WITH A CHILD

*Notes*    **General discussion of both Elements (2)(a) and (2)(b),** *p. 91*: A defendant's acts of inserting his tongue in the mouths of two children while kissing them and inserting his tongue in their eyes and noses after getting in bed with them satisfied both Elements (2)(a) and (2)(b) (322 N.C. 753).

# 8

# Robbery, Blackmail, Extortion, and Kidnapping

## COMMON LAW ROBBERY

*Notes*  **Lesser-included offenses** [new note to be inserted after **Multiple victims**], *p. 95*: Larceny is a lesser-included offense of robbery (322 N.C. 506; 305 N.C. 391).

## ARMED ROBBERY

*Notes*  **Element (3),** *p. 96*: The statement about the effect of a victim's perception that a robber appears to be using a dangerous weapon should be clarified. If it appears to the victim that a robber is using a dangerous weapon and no evidence to the contrary is presented, then the jury must find that the robber used a dangerous weapon that threatened or endangered the victim's life. If contrary evidence is presented, the jury may still infer the use of a dangerous weapon that threatened or endangered the victim's life (312 N.C. 779). In one case, a glass vase was held to be a dangerous weapon as used by the defendant (313 N.C. 554). Even if a dangerous weapon was neither seen at the time of the offense nor found later, the use of a dangerous weapon may be inferred from the victim's testimony about being hit with an object and from the nature of the victim's wound (87 N.C. App. 246).

**Timing of elements** [new note to be inserted after **Element (4)**], *p. 97*: Evidence is sufficient for armed robbery even if the victim is dead when the property is taken, as long as the offense is committed under circumstances and in a time frame such that the robbery and the victim's death occur during a single transaction (315 N.C. 191). Evidence is sufficient for armed robbery even if the defendant's intent to steal is formed after the use or threat of force, as long as the theft and use or threat of force occur during a single transaction (315 N.C. 191; 319 N.C. 577; 321 N.C. 594). Evidence is sufficient for armed robbery as long as the use or threat of force occurs before or with the theft or during the same time as the theft to constitute a single transaction (317 N.C. 302).

**Lesser-included offenses** [new note to be inserted after **Multiple victims**], *p. 97*: Common law robbery and larceny are lesser-included offenses of armed robbery (322 N.C. 506; 312 N.C. 779).

# EXTORTION

*Notes*    **Element (1),** *p. 100*: A defendant was properly convicted of this offense when he demanded specific sums of money from the victim in return for agreeing not to bring criminal charges against the victim (92 N.C. App. 563).

# FIRST-DEGREE KIDNAPPING

*Notes*    **Multiple punishment,** *p. 102*: A defendant may not be convicted of both first-degree kidnapping and rape if the rape is the factor that elevates the offense from second-degree to first-degree kidnapping, and if the jury does not find another factor—such as the defendant's failure to release the victim in a safe place—that would elevate the kidnapping to first-degree. In such a case the first-degree kidnapping must be reduced to a conviction of second-degree kidnapping or judgment must be arrested for the rape conviction (318 N.C. 141; 317 N.C. 283; 316 N.C. 13; 313 N.C. 297).

# FELONIOUS RESTRAINT

[This is a new crime enacted by Chapter 545 of the Session Laws of 1985, to be inserted after **SECOND-DEGREE KIDNAPPING,** *p. 103*.]

*Statute*    **§ 14-43.3. Felonious restraint.**

   A person commits the offense of felonious restraint if he unlawfully restrains another person without that person's consent, or the consent of the person's parent or legal custodian if the person is less than 16 years old, and moves the person from the place of the initial restraint by transporting him in a motor vehicle or other conveyance. Violation of this section is a Class J felony. Felonious restraint is considered a lesser included offense of kidnapping.

*Elements*    A person is guilty of this offense if that person:
(1) unlawfully restrains a person
(2) without the person's consent (or, if the person is under sixteen, without the consent of the person's parent or guardian)
(3) by transporting the person by motor vehicle or other conveyance from the place of the initial restraint.

*Punishment*    Class J felony punishable by maximum imprisonment of three years and/or a fine (presumptive sentence one year).

*Notes*    **In general.** The law creating this offense does not expressly or by implication abolish the common law crime of false imprisonment.

**Lesser-included offenses.** G.S. 14-43.3 expressly states that this offense is a lesser-included offense of kidnapping.

---

# FALSE IMPRISONMENT

*Notes*    **Element (3),** *p. 104*: To prove that the restraint was against the victim's will, the prosecution must show that the defendant used actual force, threatened force, or fraud resulting in coerced consent (278 N.C. 42; 73 N.C. App. 546).

# 9

# Burglary and Breaking or Entering

---

## FIRST-DEGREE BURGLARY

*Notes*    **Element (1),** *p. 107*: The breaking of an inner door of a house or apartment can satisfy this element (313 N.C. 539).

**Element (5),** *p. 108*: Although a spouse generally cannot be convicted of burglary or breaking or entering for breaking into the other spouse's dwelling or of larceny for taking the other spouse's property, such a conviction is proper if the evidence shows that the other spouse had exclusive possession of the dwelling and of the property taken (81 N.C. App. 490; 73 N.C. App. 432).

**Element (8),** *p. 109*: If the intruder does not form the intent to commit a felony or larceny until after he or she breaks and enters, the offense is misdemeanor breaking or entering rather than burglary (313 N.C. 554). The mere fact that an intruder broke and entered at nighttime a dwelling occupied by a woman does not suffice to prove intent to rape (307 N.C. 445; 90 N.C. App. 185).

**Doctrine of possession of recently stolen property,** *p. 109*: An interval of thirty days between the discovery of theft of someone's property—a television set, towels, linens, and a fan—and the location of the stolen items in the defendant's possession did not support an inference of breaking or entering and larceny, since the items stolen were of a type normally and frequently traded through lawful channels (316 N.C. 41). An interval of eleven to twelve days between the larceny and the defendant's possession of commercial restaurant equipment did support an inference of breaking or entering and larceny because such equipment is not usually or frequently traded through lawful channels (83 N.C. App. 323). Similarly, an interval of nine days between the larceny and the defendant's possession of unique tools and metal work supported an inference of breaking or entering and larceny (86 N.C. App. 235).

---

# SECOND-DEGREE BURGLARY

*Notes*   **Element (4),** *p. 110*: An unoccupied toolshed located forty-five feet from the dwelling was not within the curtilage and therefore an entry into the toolshed was not second-degree burglary (315 N.C. 191).

# BREAKING OR ENTERING VEHICLE

*Notes*   **Proof of personal property within vehicle** [new note to be inserted after **Definitions**], *p. 117*: Element (4) of *I. Breaking or Entering Vehicle*, and Element (3) of *II. Breaking Out of Vehicle*, require proof that a vehicle contained personal property of some value, however, trivial (such as a vehicle registration card, hubcap key, papers, cigarettes, or a shoe bag) (321 N.C. 267).

# 10
# Arson

## FIRST-DEGREE ARSON

*Notes*     **Element (3),** *p. 125*: When one occupant of the dwelling had been murdered several days before the burning of the dwelling and the other occupant had permanently abandoned the dwelling, the dwelling was not inhabited (93 N.C. App. 682).

# 11

# Trespass and Property Damage

## TRESPASS AFTER BEING FORBIDDEN, *p. 140*:

[This offense was repealed by Chapter 700 of the Session Laws of 1987.]

## FIRST-DEGREE TRESPASS

[This is a new offense enacted by Chapter 700 of the Session Laws of 1987, to be inserted in place of **TRESPASS AFTER BEING FORBIDDEN,** *p. 140*.]

*Statute*

**§ 14-159.12. First degree trespass.**

    (a) Offense.—A person commits the offense of first degree trespass if, without authorization, he enters or remains:
        (1) On premises of another so enclosed or secured as to demonstrate clearly an intent to keep out intruders; or
        (2) In a building of another.
    (b) Classification.—First degree trespass is a misdemeanor punishable by imprisonment for up to six months, a fine of up to one thousand dollars ($1,000), or both.

*Elements*

A person is guilty of this offense if that person:
(1) without authorization
(2) (a) enters, *or*
    (b) remains
(3) (a) on premises of another so enclosed or secured as to demonstrate an intent to keep out intruders, *or*
    (b) in a building of another.

*Punishment*

Misdemeanor punishable by maximum imprisonment of six months and/or a maximum fine of $1,000.

*Notes*

**In general.** The basic distinction between first- and second-degree trespass is the strength of interests in privacy, possession, and control of premises protected by the offenses. The crime of first-degree trespass involves stronger interests and, therefore, more serious violations of privacy, possession, and control of premises. This offense also prohibits many of the same acts (at least those of entering) that are prohibited by MISDEMEANOR BREAKING OR ENTERING OF BUILDING—see page 113 of the book.

**Element (1).** Without authorization probably means the same as without consent in breaking or entering offenses—see page 112 of the book. The possessor may exclude a person for any reason (247 N.C. 455) except one that rests on a basis (such as race) that is prohibited by federal civil rights laws.

**Element (2).** See page 107 of the book for the definition of "entering." "Remains" means *stays*. It is an affirmative defense to trespass that a defendant entered with reasonable grounds to believe in a legal right to enter, even though the defendant did not have a legal right to enter (231 N.C. 136; 170 N.C. 737).

**Element (3)(a).** Premises include the entire piece of real estate—the building and the land. A fenced-in area surrounding all or a part of the premises may satisfy this element.

**Element (3)(b).** This offense is committed if a person enters a building (home, business, etc.) after previously having been forbidden or remains after having been ordered to leave. Thus, this offense is essentially the same as the now-repealed TRESPASS AFTER BEING FORBIDDEN (G.S. 14-134), when the trespass involves the entering or remaining in a building without authorization. For example, if a homeowner tells the defendant—when the defendant is inside his or her house—to leave, and the defendant refuses to do so, or if the homeowner tells the defendant never to come back onto this property again but the defendant comes back and enters the homeowner's house, the defendant has committed first-degree trespass. G.S. 14-159.11 defines "building" as any structure or part of a structure, other than a conveyance, enclosed so as to permit reasonable entry only through a door and roofed to protect it from the elements.

**Spouse forbidding entry to spouse.** Applying the law of trespass in domestic disputes has been particularly difficult because of the problem of determining ownership or custody of the property. The offense of DOMESTIC CRIMINAL TRESPASS, discussed in the book on page 142, usually will be the more appropriate charge to consider.

**Invitation by tenant after forbidding by landlord.** Unless the tenant's lease denies the tenant the authority to invite, a guest who enters premises at the invitation of the tenant is not guilty of this offense even if the landlord has told the guest not to enter (101 N.C. 717).

**Asserting rights of free speech on shopping mall property.** A defendant was properly convicted of trespass when he refused to leave the parking lot of a shopping mall after he was asked to stop soliciting signatures against the draft. The mall parking lot was private property, and it had not been dedicated to public use in a way that would guarantee rights to free speech under federal or state constitutions (302 N.C. 173).

**Lesser-included offenses.** G.S. 14-159.14 provides that first- and second-degree trespass are lesser-included offenses of breaking or entering in G.S. 14-54 (felonious and misdemeanor breaking or entering building) and G.S. 14-56 (felonious breaking or entering motor vehicle, railroad car, etc.), even though there appears to be no difference in the elements of misdemeanor breaking or entering under G.S. 14-54(b) and first-degree trespass with respect to unauthorized entry of a building.

# SECOND-DEGREE TRESPASS

[This is a new offense enacted by Chapter 700 of the Session Laws of 1987, to be inserted after **FIRST-DEGREE TRESPASS**, *p. 140*.]

*Statute*

### § 14-159.13. Second degree trespass.

(a) Offense.—A person commits the offense of second degree trespass if, without authorization, he enters or remains on premises of another:

(1) After he has been notified not to enter or remain there by the owner, by a person in charge of the premises, by a lawful occupant, or by another authorized person; or

(2) That are posted, in a manner reasonably likely to come to the attention of intruders, with notice not to enter the premises.

(b) Classification.—Second degree trespass is a misdemeanor punishable by imprisonment for up to 30 days, a fine up to two hundred dollars ($200.00), or both.

*Elements*

A person is guilty of this offense if that person:

(1) without authorization

(2) (a) enters, *or*

    (b) remains

(3) on premises of another

(4) (a) after having been notified not to enter or remain there by the owner, a person in charge of premises, a lawful occupant, or another authorized person, *or*

    (b) when the premises are posted, in a manner reasonably likely to come to the attention of intruders, with notice not to enter the premises.

*Punishment*

Misdemeanor punishable by maximum imprisonment of thirty days and/or a maximum fine of $200.

*Notes*

**Elements (1) and (2).** See the notes for Elements (1) and (2) under FIRST-DEGREE TRESPASS.

**Element (3).** Premises include the entire piece of real estate—the building and the land.

**Element (4)(a).** This element makes second-degree trespass the same as the now-repealed TRESPASS AFTER BEING FORBIDDEN (G.S. 14-134). For example, if a homeowner tells the defendant to leave the homeowner's front yard and the defendant refuses, or if the homeowner tells the defendant never to come back onto the homeowner's property again but the defendant enters the property, the defendant has committed second-degree trespass. However, if the unauthorized entering or remaining occurs in a building, FIRST-DEGREE TRESPASS should be charged. "Another authorized person" could include an agent of the owner or occupant of the premises.

**Element (4)(b).** This element may be satisfied by posting "No trespassing" or similar signs in a manner reasonably likely to come to an intruder's attention. Proof that the intruder actually saw the signs is not required.

**Lesser-included offenses.** G.S. 14-159.14 provides that first- and second-degree trespass are lesser-included offenses of breaking or entering in G.S. 14-54 (felonious and misdemeanor breaking or entering building) and G.S. 14-56 (felonious breaking or entering motor vehicle, railroad car, etc.).

*Related offenses not in this chapter*

See the related offenses under FIRST-DEGREE TRESPASS.

# FORCIBLE ENTRY AND DETAINER, *p. 144*:

[This offense was repealed by Chapter 700 of the Session Laws of 1987.]

# INJURY TO PERSONAL PROPERTY

*Notes*

**Element (2),** *p. 151*: The statement in this note is incorrect. The statute specifies that personal property need *not* be destroyed for a violation to occur.

# 12

# Larceny, Embezzlement, and Related Offenses

## MISDEMEANOR LARCENY

*Notes* **Element (1),** *p. 155*: To be sufficient, an indictment for larceny must allege the identity of the owner of the property or the identity of the person in lawful possession of the property (such as the possessor, bailee, or other person with a special property interest in the stolen property) and the evidence must support the allegation. Proof of mere ownership of the premises from which property is stolen does not by itself establish ownership or possession of, or interest in, the stolen property (313 N.C. 164).

**Element (3),** *p. 155*: Larceny violates the right to possess property, not the right to own it. Thus, even the owner of property may be guilty of larceny if the owner steals his or her property that is in another person's lawful possession (*Perkins*, page 297).

**Taking livestock and dogs,** *p. 156*: Chapter 773 of the Session Laws of 1989 amended G.S. 14-81 to add a provision that larceny of a dog is a Class J felony (maximum imprisonment three years, presumptive sentence one year) regardless of the value of the dog taken. Larceny of horses, mules, swine, or cattle remains a Class H felony.

**Doctrine of possession of recently stolen property,** *p. 156*: Use of the doctrine requires proof that the stolen property was found in the defendant's custody and had been in the defendant's possession or subject to his or her control and disposition since the theft (313 N.C. 516). The doctrine was applied in a case in which the defendant or his girlfriend possessed a stolen watch for up to four weeks after it was stolen (313 N.C. 516). It was also applied in a case in which the defendant possessed commercial restaurant equipment eleven to twelve days after it had been stolen, since such property is not usually traded in lawful retail channels (83 N.C. App. 323).

## FELONIOUS LARCENY

*Notes* **Element (6)(a),** *p. 158*: The proper measure of the value of a stolen item is its fair market value at the time of the theft, not its replacement cost. The fair market value must be established by direct evidence, not by mere speculation (318 N.C. 643; 318 N.C. 602).

# LARCENY OF CHOSE IN ACTION

*Notes*    **Chose in action,** *p. 159*: See 75 N.C. 257 concerning the common law rule. A blank check appears not to be a chose in action under this statute. Because a blank check has at least some value, however trivial, the theft of a blank check can be charged as misdemeanor larceny. Although no North Carolina case has addressed this issue, see a New Jersey case, 113 N.J. Super. 1, 272 A.2d 539 (1971).

# RECEIVING STOLEN GOODS— MISDEMEANOR

*Notes*    **Element (3),** *p. 162*: Add 316 N.C. 295 as an additional citation to the case citations in this note on the meaning of "reasonable grounds to believe."

**Element (4),** *p. 162*: The element of dishonest purpose in receiving or possessing stolen goods may be shown by evidence that the receiver or possessor acted with intent to aid the thief (or receiver or possessor) of the goods; it is irrelevant that the receiver or possessor did not gain personally by his or her actions (316 N.C. 295).

# RECEIVING STOLEN GOODS FELONIOUSLY, *p. 163*:

See the notes in this supplement under RECEIVING STOLEN GOODS—MISDEMEANOR.

# MISDEMEANOR POSSESSION OF STOLEN GOODS, *p. 164*:

See the notes in this supplement under RECEIVING STOLEN GOODS—MISDEMEANOR.

*Notes*    **Generally,** *p. 165*: If a defendant is found to possess more than one stolen item, the number of separate offenses of possession of stolen property for which the defendant may be convicted equals the number of times the defendant obtained possession of the property. Thus, if a defendant obtains ten stolen items during eight different episodes of receipt, the defendant is guilty of eight separate offenses of possession of stolen goods (322 N.C. 770).

# FELONIOUS POSSESSION OF STOLEN GOODS, *p. 165*:

See the notes in this supplement under RECEIVING STOLEN GOODS—MISDEMEANOR.

---

# SHOPLIFTING—CONCEALING MERCHANDISE

*Punishment, p. 169*: [Chapter 841 of the Session Laws of 1986 and Chapter 660 of the Session Laws of 1987 established a new punishment schedule for this offense and the following one, **SHOPLIFTING—SUBSTITUTION OF PRICE**, provided below.]

(1) For the first offense or for a subsequent offense not covered by the repeat offender provisions below, imprisonment of twenty-four hours to sixty days and a maximum fine of $100 (the court may suspend the term of imprisonment on condition that the defendant perform at least twenty-four hours of community service);

(2) For the second offense committed within three years of a conviction under G.S. 14-72.1, imprisonment of seventy-two hours to six months and a maximum fine of $500 (the court may suspend the term of imprisonment on condition that the defendant be imprisoned for at least seventy-two hours, or perform at least seventy-two hours of community service, or both);

(3) For the third or subsequent offense committed within five years of two previous convictions under G.S. 14-72.1, imprisonment of fourteen days to two years and a fine (the court may suspend the term of imprisonment on condition that the defendant be imprisoned for at least fourteen days).

If a judge finds that a defendant is unable, due to mental or physical disability, to perform community service, the judge may impose a different appropriate sentence.

If a court imposes an active term of imprisonment under G.S. 14-72.1, it is subject to the following limitations:

(1) The court may not give the defendant credit for the first twenty-four hours of incarceration pending trial;

(2) Neither good time nor gain time may reduce the mandatory minimum period of imprisonment; and

(3) The defendant may not be released or paroled unless otherwise eligible and he has served the mandatory minimum period of imprisonment.

---

# SHOPLIFTING—SUBSTITUTION OF PRICE

*Punishment, p. 170*: See the discussion in this supplement (above) of the revised punishment for SHOPLIFTING—CONCEALING MERCHANDISE, which also applies to this offense.

# EMBEZZLEMENT

*Notes*    **Element (3),** *p. 177*: A partner cannot be guilty under G.S. 14-90 of embezzlement of partnership funds; instead, the partner may be prosecuted for appropriating partnership funds to personal use which violates G.S. 14-97 (81 N.C. App. 281).

**Distinction between embezzlement and malfeasance of a corporate agent** [new note to be added after **Element (4)**], *p. 177*: Although the offense of embezzlement and that of malfeasance of a corporate agent (G.S. 14-254) may arise from the same conduct, there are significant differences in the definitions of these two similar offenses: (a) to be convicted of embezzlement, a defendant must have received property in the course of employment while acting in a fiduciary capacity, whereas to be convicted of malfeasance (G.S. 14-254), a defendant need only have taken or misapplied any property of the corporation for which he or she is an agent; (b) to be guilty of embezzlement, a defendant must have intended to defraud his or her principal, whereas G.S. 14-254 covers intent to defraud any person; and (c) to be guilty of embezzlement, a defendant need not be an agent or fiduciary of a corporation, whereas G.S. 14-254 applies only to agents or fiduciaries of corporations (313 N.C. 1).

# EMBEZZLEMENT OF STATE PROPERTY BY PUBLIC OFFICERS AND EMPLOYEES

*Notes*    **Element (4),** *p. 178*: A defendant's authority to hire school instructors as provided in the school's budget did not entrust him with the funds used to pay the instructors and therefore he did not commit this offense (however, because he obtained the funds by a deceptive scheme, he probably committed the offense of obtaining property by false pretenses) (91 N.C. App. 424).

# 13

# Fraud, Forgery, and Related Offenses

## WORTHLESS CHECK—MAKING OR UTTERING

*Notes*     **Use of affidavits at hearing or trial** [new note to be inserted after **Similar Offenses**], *p. 184*: Subsections (a) through (e) of G.S. 14-107.1 provide that an affidavit (satisfying the statute's detailed requirements) of a person accepting a check is admissible as prima facie evidence in a prosecution of a violation of G.S. 14-107 to establish that the defendant was the person who passed the check; the check also may be introduced with its markings (for example, "insufficient funds") as prima facie evidence of the reason why the bank did not accept it. This prima facie evidence rule does not apply unless the affidavit has been filed before issuance of the initial charge.

G.S. 14-107.1(f) provides that an affidavit of a bank employee is admissible at a district court hearing or trial to prove the reason for dishonor of the check, such as whether there were sufficient funds in the account or other related matters. The defendant must be provided with a copy of the affidavit before trial and have the opportunity to subpoena the affiant for trial.

## OBTAINING PROPERTY FOR WORTHLESS CHECK

*Notes*     **Element (4),** *p. 186*: Contrary to the statement in this note, any other "thing" of value could fairly be interpreted to include services.

# OBTAINING PROPERTY BY FALSE PRETENSES

*Notes*

**Elements (1), (2), and (3),** *p. 187*: Although a false promise to perform an act in the future may satisfy the requirement that a defendant made a false representation with intent to defraud, proof that a defendant failed to fulfill a contractual duty through ineptness or lack of diligence is not sufficient to satisfy these elements (90 N.C. App. 101).

**Element (5),** *p. 188*: A defendant who told a car salesman that she wanted to test drive a car after falsely representing her identity was properly convicted of obtaining property by false pretenses after she drove the car away and did not return it (75 N.C. App. 461).

# FRAUDULENT DISPOSAL OF SECURITY, *p. 190*:

[This statute was revised by Chapter 1065 of the Session Laws of 1987 (Regular Session 1988).]

*Statute*

## § 14-114. Fraudulent disposal of personal property on which there is a security interest.

(a) If any person, after executing a security agreement on personal property for a lawful purpose, shall make any disposition of any property embraced in such security agreement, with intent to defeat the rights of the secured party, every person so offending and every person with a knowledge of the security interest buying any property embraced in which security agreement, and every person assisting, aiding or abetting the unlawful disposition of such property, with intent to defeat the rights of any secured party in such security agreement, shall be guilty of a misdemeanor punishable by a fine not to exceed five hundred dollars ($500.00), imprisonment for not more than six months, or both.

A person's refusal to turn over secured property to a secured party who is attempting to repossess the property without a judgment or order for possession shall not, by itself, be a violation of this section.

(b) Intent to commit the crime as set forth in subsection (a) may be presumed from proof of possession of the property embraced in such security agreement by the grantor thereof after execution of the security agreement, and while it is in force, the further proof of the fact that the sheriff or other officer charged with the execution of process cannot after due diligence find such property under process directed to him for its seizure, for the satisfaction of such security agreement. However, this presumption may be rebutted by evidence that the property has, through no fault of the defendant, been stolen, lost, damaged beyond repair, or otherwise disposed of by the defendant without intent to defeat the rights of the secured party.

*Elements*

A person is guilty of this offense if that person:
(1) executes a security agreement on personal property for a lawful purpose
(2) and while the security agreement is in force the person disposes of property "embraced in the security agreement" or assists, aids, or abets the disposition of such property
(3) with the intent to defeat the rights of the secured party.

*Punishment*

Misdemeanor punishable by maximum imprisonment of six months and/or a maximum fine of $500.

*Notes*    **In general.** The statute provides that a person's refusal to turn over secured property to a secured party who is attempting to repossess the property without a judgment or order for possession is not, by itself, a violation of the statute.

**Element (1).** A security agreement is a written agreement that makes specified personal property subject to being claimed by another to whom the owner owes money if the owner should fail to make good on the debt. Any property to which the agreement refers is "embraced" in the agreement.

**Element (2).** It is not necessary to prove the identity of the person to whom the property was conveyed.

**Evidence rule.** The statute provides that the intent to commit the offense may be inferred (a) from proof of possession of the property embraced in the security agreement by the grantor after execution of the security agreement, and (b) from the fact that, while the agreement is in force, the sheriff or other officer executing process cannot after due diligence find the property under the process directing the officer to seize it to satisfy the agreement. This inference may be rebutted by evidence that the property has, through no fault of the defendant, been stolen, lost, damaged beyond repair, or otherwise disposed of by the defendant without the intent to defeat the rights of the secured party.

*Related offenses not in this chapter*    ALTERING OR REMOVING SERIAL NUMBERS (Chapter 12)
Failure to make payment out of designated property (G.S. 14-105)

---

# FRAUDULENT PURCHASE OF SECURITY

*Elements, p. 191*:    (3) As a result of changes made by Chapter 1065 of the Session Laws of 1987 (Regular Session, 1988), this element should read:
"with intent to defeat the rights of the secured party."

---

# SECRETING PROPERTY TO HINDER ENFORCEMENT OF SECURITY INTEREST,
*p. 192*:

[This statute was revised by Chapter 1065 of the Session Laws of 1987 (Regular Session, 1988) and Chapter 401 of the Session Laws of 1989.]

*Statute*    **§ 14-115. Secreting property to hinder enforcement of lien or security interest.**

Any person with intent to prevent or hinder the enforcement of the lien or security interest after a judgment or order has been issued for possession for that personal property subject to said lien or security interest either refuses to surrender such personal property in his possession to a law enforcement officer, or removes, or exchanges, or secretes such personal property shall be guilty of a misdemeanor punishable by a fine not to exceed five hundred dollars ($500.00), imprisonment for not more than six months, or both.

*Elements, p. 192*:      [The elements should read as follows.]

A person is guilty of this offense if that person:

(1) (a) removes, exchanges, or secretes personal property *or*

    (b) refuses to surrender to a law enforcement officer personal property in that person's possession

(2) on which a lien or security interest exists

(3) after a judgment or order for possession has been issued for possession for that personal property

(4) with intent to prevent or hinder the enforcement of the lien or security interest.

# FORGERY

*Notes*      **Element (1),** *p. 193*: The correct citation of the first case in this note is 94 N.C. 836. Also, regarding the inference of forgery from possession of a forged instrument, a jury instruction was unconstitutional when it stated that a person who possesses a forged instrument and endeavors to obtain money with it is *presumed* to have forged or consented to its forgery, when the jury reasonably would have interpreted the presumption to be a conclusive or mandatory presumption; that presumption unconstitutionally shifted the burden of proof to the defendant (702 F. Supp. 1240). An instruction on a permissive presumption or inference, where the jury could choose to accept or reject the presumption or inference, would be constitutional.

# FINANCIAL TRANSACTION CARD FRAUD

*Statute, p. 200*:      Chapter 161 of the Session Laws of 1989 added a new subsection (c1) to G.S. 14-113.13 to make it a misdemeanor punishable by a maximum imprisonment of one year and/or a maximum fine of $1,000 when a person (who is authorized to accept a financial transaction card or account number for goods and services) submits to the card-issuing financial institution or business organization a record of a sale that was not made and does so with the intent to defraud. Chapter 161 also added a new statute, G.S. 14-113.15A, to make it a Class J felony, punishable by a maximum imprisonment of three years (presumptive sentence one year) and/or a fine when a person solicits a merchant to remit for payment a record of a sale (involving a financial transaction card) that was not made.

# FOOD STAMP FRAUD

## I. Fraudulently Obtaining or Transferring Food Stamps

*Elements, p. 211*:

[The elements should be corrected to read as follows.]

A person is guilty of this offense if that person:

(1) knowingly

(2) (a) (i) obtains *or* attempts to obtain *or* aids and abets any person to obtain

(ii) by means of willfully making a false representation *or* by impersonation *or* by failing to disclose material facts, *or*

(b) transfers with intent to defraud in any manner not authorized by the food stamp statutes (G.S. Ch. 108A, Art. 2, Part 5) and associated regulations

(3) food stamps or authorization cards

(4) to which the person is not entitled.

# 14

# Disorderly Conduct and Riot

## DISORDERLY CONDUCT

*III. Disorderly Conduct by Seizing or Blocking a School Building*

*Notes*  **Generally,** *p. 222*: Chapter 671 of the Session Laws of 1987 clarified G.S. 14-288.4(a)(4)a. concerning disorderly conduct by refusing to vacate a building or facility of an educational institution when ordered to do so by the institution's chief administrative officer or his representative. The act specified that for colleges and universities, such a representative includes the vice chancellor for student affairs or equivalent, the dean of students or equivalent, and the director and chief of the campus law enforcement or security department.

## DEMONSTRATION IN PUBLIC BUILDING, *p. 225*:

[This offense was repealed by Chapter 700 of the Session Laws of 1987.]

## BLOCKING PUBLIC BUILDING, *p. 226*:

[This offense was repealed by Chapter 700 of the Session Laws of 1987.]

# 15

# Crimes against the Administration of Justice

## RESISTING, DELAYING, OR OBSTRUCTING AN OFFICER

*Notes*   **Element (2),** *p. 246*: This statute prohibits communications intended to hinder or prevent an officer from carrying out an official duty, though not communications intended to express disagreement or criticism, to clarify a misunderstanding, or to obtain information. A conviction was proper in a case in which two defendants, despite being ordered to halt, approached within six feet of officers who were trying to arrest a man on a narcotics charge and began to shout; one defendant raised his fists into the air and shouted, "No, no, no, he ain't going nowhere," and the other yelled, "Stop it, he ain't going." The court concluded that the defendants' conduct showed their determination to prevent the officers from arresting the man and that their acts caused the officers temporarily to lose control of him (73 N.C. App. 612).

**Element (3),** *p. 246*: In a case involving an assault on a law enforcement officer that would likely apply also to this offense, the North Carolina Supreme Court ruled that the state must prove that the defendant knew that the person he was assaulting was a law enforcement officer (315 N.C. 1).

## ESCAPE OR ATTEMPTING TO ESCAPE FROM STATE PRISON SYSTEM

*Notes*   **Element (2),** *p. 249*: Chapter 226 of the Session Laws of 1985 made a technical change by repealing the criminal prohibitions in G.S. 148-45(a)(3) and (b)(3) against escape by a person convicted of a misdemeanor or felony who has been committed to state prison pending appeal under former G.S. 15-183. This change conforms G.S. 148-45 to the repeal of G.S. 15-183 by Chapter 711 of the Session Laws of 1977. Since G.S. 15A-1353(a) provides that a prison sentence begins when the court issues an order of commitment, subdivisions (a)(1) and (b)(1) of G.S. 148-45 now cover escapes of prisoners who are serving prison sentences pending appeal.

# 16

# Weapons Offenses

## POSSESSION OF FIREARM BY FELON

*Elements, p. 255*:

(1)(a) [Chapter 770 of the Session Laws of 1989 added a conviction of a felony in Article 7A (rape, sexual offense and other crimes) as a prohibition against possessing a firearm.]

*Notes*

**Element (2),** *p. 255*: The exception from criminal liability for possession of a firearm in one's own home does not apply to possession of a firearm in the common areas of a motel (83 N.C. App. 529) or apartment house—such as stairways, halls, and parks (78 N.C. App. 514).

**Element (3),** *p. 255*: The prosecution need not prove the barrel length or overall length of a handgun; these measurements are only elements for possession of other kinds of firearms (83 N.C. App. 529).

**Broader federal firearms statute,** *p. 256*: [Congress has repealed 18 U.S. Code, Appendix II §§ 1201, 1202, and 1203; therefore, substitute the following discussion for that contained in the book.]

A federal statute, 18 U.S. Code § 921(g), prohibits the possession, receipt, or transportation in interstate commerce of any firearm by a person who has been convicted in any state or federal court of a crime punishable by more than one year's imprisonment. However, 18 U.S.C. § 921(a)(20) excludes a conviction in a state of an offense classified by that state as a misdemeanor and punishable by a maximum of two years imprisonment or less, a conviction for certain offenses relating to the regulation of business practices, and a conviction which has been expunged, set aside, or for which the person has been pardoned or has had civil rights restored (see G.S. 13-1), unless the pardon, expungement, or civil rights restoration expressly provides that the person may not ship, transport, possess, or receive firearms. The federal statute also prohibits the possession, receipt, or transportation in interstate commerce of any firearm by a person who is a fugitive from justice, who is a narcotics user or addict, who has been adjudged mentally defective or has been committed to a mental institution, who is an illegal alien, who has been dishonorably discharged from the armed forces, or who has renounced United States citizenship. "Firearm" in 18 U.S.C. § 921(a)(3) is defined to include any weapon (including a starter gun) which will or is designed to or may readily be converted to expel a projectile by the action of an explosive, the frame or receiver of any such weapon, any firearm muffler or silencer, or any destructive device, with the exception of antique firearms. Note that this federal law is broader than G.S. 14-415.1: it includes all firearms (handgun, rifle, shotgun) with no restrictions as to barrel length, and there is no time limit on its prohibition of firearm possession by convicted felons. However, a convicted felon can obtain relief from the federal prohibitions by applying under 18 U.S.C. § 925(c) to the Secretary of the Treasury for permission to possess firearms; this is done by applying to the Alcohol, Tobacco, and Firearms Bureau of the U.S. Treasury Department (ATF). Note that no such relief is possible with the prohibition imposed by G.S. 14-415.1.

# CARRYING CONCEALED WEAPON, *p. 257*:

[The statute below includes changes made by Chapter 432 of the Session Laws of 1985.]

*Statute*  **§ 14-269. Carrying concealed weapons.**

(a) It shall be unlawful for any person, except when on his own premises, willfully and intentionally to carry concealed about his person any bowie knife, dirk, dagger, slung shot, loaded cane, metallic knuckles, razor, shurikin, stun gun, pistol, gun or other deadly weapon of like kind. This section does not apply to an ordinary pocket knife carried in a closed position. As used in this section, "ordinary pocket knife" means a small knife, designed for carrying in a pocket or purse, which has its cutting edge and point entirely enclosed by its handle, and that may not be opened by a throwing, explosive or spring action.

(b) This prohibition shall not apply to the following persons:
(1) Officers and enlisted personnel of the armed forces of the United States when in discharge of their official duties as such and acting under orders requiring them to carry arms and weapons;
(2) Civil officers of the United States while in the discharge of their official duties;
(3) Officers and soldiers of the militia and the national guard when called into actual service;
(4) Officers of the State, or of any county, city, or town, charged with the execution of the laws of the State, when acting in the discharge of their official duties;
(5) Full-time sworn law-enforcement officers, when off-duty, in the jurisdiction where they are assigned, if:
a. Written regulations authorizing the carrying of concealed weapons have been filed with the clerk of superior court in the county where the law-enforcement unit is located by the sheriff or chief of police or other superior officer in charge; and
b. Such regulations specifically prohibit the carrying of concealed weapons while the officer is consuming or under the influence of alcoholic beverages.

(b1) It is a defense to a prosecution under this section that:
(1) The weapon was not a firearm;
(2) The defendant was engaged in, or on the way to or from, an activity in which he legitimately used the weapon;
(3) The defendant possessed the weapon for that legitimate use; and
(4) The defendant did not use or attempt to use the weapon for an illegal purpose.
The burden of proving this defense is on the defendant.

(c) Any person violating the provisions of this section shall be guilty of a misdemeanor, and shall be punished by a fine not to exceed five hundred dollars ($500.00), imprisonment for not more than six months, or both.

*Elements, p. 257*:      (5) Shurikins (star-shaped martial arts throwing weapons) and stun guns have been added to the list of designated weapons.

*Notes*      **Element (3), *p. 257***: A conviction was affirmed when a police officer found a gun under the driver's seat of a car driven by the defendant, in which the defendant was seen to reach under the seat as though placing something there after an accident (75 N.C. App. 637). In contrast, evidence was found insufficient for a conviction when a defendant was in the driver's seat of a car and a gun was found under the back seat (273 N.C. 620). A weapon probably is not concealed if it is partly exposed to view (121 N.C. 556; but see 187 N.C. 477).

**Ordinary pocket knife not prohibited** [new note to be added before **Disposition of weapons**], *p. 258*: This offense does not apply to an ordinary pocket knife carried in a closed position. An "ordinary pocket knife" is defined as a small knife, designed for carrying in a pocket or purse, which has its cutting edge and point entirely enclosed by its handle and which may not be opened by a throwing, explosive, or spring action.

**Affirmative defense** [new note to be added before **Disposition of weapons**], *p. 258*: It is a defense to a prosecution of this offense that the weapon was not a firearm, and that the defendant was engaged in or on the way to or from an activity involving a legitimate use of the weapon and that the defendant possessed the weapon for that legitimate use and did not use or attempt to use the weapon for an illegal purpose.

---

# MANUFACTURE, POSSESSION, ETC., OF MACHINE GUN, SAWED-OFF SHOTGUN, OR WEAPON OF MASS DESTRUCTION

*Notes*      **Constitutionality** [new note to be inserted after **Persons exempted**], *p. 264*: The prohibition against possessing a sawed-off shotgun does not violate the United States or North Carolina constitutions (95 N.C. App. 140).

**Inoperability of weapon is affirmative defense** [new note to be inserted after **Persons exempted**], *p. 264*: Possessing an inoperable weapon does not constitute an offense under this law. However, the state need not prove the weapon's operability unless the defendant offers evidence of its inoperability (95 N.C. App. 140).

# 17

# Crimes against Sexual Morality

## CRIME AGAINST NATURE

*Notes*  **Comparison with taking indecent liberties,** *p. 267*: Crime against nature also differs from G.S. 14-27.7, which prohibits sexual activity by a substitute parent. Penetration of or by the sexual organ is an essential element of crime against nature, but not of sexual activity by a substitute parent. In addition, G.S. 14-27.7 requires that the sexual act be performed by a person who has "assumed the role of parent" to the victim. That requirement is not an element of crime against nature (89 N.C. App. 199).

## Obscenity Offenses

### OBSCENITY: DEFINITIONS AND CIVIL HEARING—OBSCENITY: PUBLIC DISPLAY OF SEXUALLY ORIENTED MATERIALS, *pp. 273–85*:

Delete all material in the book on these pages and replace it with the following seventeen new offenses, from **DISSEMINATING OBSCENITY** to **PERMITTING MULTIPLE OCCUPANCY IN VIEWING BOOTH.** In 1985 the General Assembly substantially revised the statutes governing obscenity, child protection, and adult establishment offenses. Of the statutes discussed on these pages, the legislature repealed G.S. 14-190.2, -190.3, -190.10, and -190.11, and it revised G.S. 14-190.1, -190.5, -190.6, -190.7, -190.8, -202.10, -202.11, and -202.12. The legislature also added the following new sections: G.S. 14-190.13, -190.14, -190.15, -190.16, -190.17, -190.18, -190.19, -190.20. The following discussion was adapted from explanations of the legislative changes written by the late L. Poindexter Watts of the Institute of Government.]

# DISSEMINATING OBSCENITY

*Statute*   **§ 14-190.1. Obscene literature and exhibitions.**

(a) It shall be unlawful for any person, firm or corporation to intentionally disseminate obscenity. A person, firm or corporation disseminates obscenity within the meaning of this Article if he or it:

(1) Sells, delivers or provides or offers or agrees to sell, deliver or provide any obscene writing, picture, record or other representation or embodiment of the obscene; or

(2) Presents or directs an obscene play, dance or other performance or participates directly in that portion thereof which makes it obscene; or

(3) Publishes, exhibits or otherwise makes available anything obscene; or

(4) Exhibits, presents, rents, sells, delivers or provides; or offers or agrees to exhibit, present, rent or to provide: any obscene still or motion picture, film, filmstrip, or projection slide, or sound recording, sound tape, or sound track, or any matter or material of whatever form which is a representation, embodiment, performance, or publication of the obscene.

(b) For purposes of this Article any material is obscene if:

(1) The material depicts or describes in a patently offensive way sexual conduct specifically defined by subsection (c) of this section; and

(2) The average person applying contemporary community standards relating to the depiction or description of sexual matters would find that the material taken as a whole appeals to the prurient interest in sex; and

(3) The material lacks serious literary, artistic, political, or scientific value; and

(4) The material as used is not protected or privileged under the Constitution of the United States or the Constitution of North Carolina.

(c) As used in this Article, "sexual conduct" means:

(1) Vaginal, anal, or oral intercourse, whether actual or simulated, normal or perverted; or

(2) Masturbation, excretory functions, or lewd exhibition of uncovered genitals; or

(3) An act or condition that depicts torture, physical restraint by being fettered or bound, or flagellation of or by a nude person or a person clad in undergarments or in revealing or bizarre costume.

(d) Obscenity shall be judged with reference to ordinary adults except that it shall be judged with reference to children or other especially susceptible audiences if it appears from the character of the material or the circumstances of its dissemination to be especially designed for or directed to such children or audiences.

(e) It shall be unlawful for any person, firm or corporation to knowingly and intentionally create, buy, procure or possess obscene material with the purpose and intent of disseminating it unlawfully.

(f) It shall be unlawful for a person, firm or corporation to advertise or otherwise promote the sale of material represented or held out by said person, firm or corporation as obscene.

(g) Violation of this section is a Class J felony.

(h) Obscene material disseminated, procured, or promoted in violation of this section is contraband.

*Elements*   A person is guilty of this offense if that person:

(1) intentionally

(2) disseminates obscenity.

*Punishment*   Class J felony punishable by maximum imprisonment of three years and/or a fine (presumptive sentence one year).

*Notes*   **Element (1).** The element of intention pertains to the act of dissemination rather than the obscene character of the material or performance. Whether material is intended to be obscene is a mixed matter of fact and law. It is no defense that a defendant mistakenly thought the material was not *legally* obscene. The cases do require, however, that the defendant have knowledge of the *character or content* of the material or performance disseminated (361 U.S. 147; 322 N.C. 22; 88 N.C. App. 624; 88 N.C. App. 69; 87 N.C. App. 217; 83 N.C. App. 544, *affirmed*, 320 N.C. 485). The term "intentionally" requires that the person who disseminates do so purposefully—that is, with a more specific intent than "knowingly" or "wantonly" or "recklessly." The acts covered by the term "disseminating obscenity" will vary substantially so that the aspect of intention will require different forms of proof in different types of cases, but in each instance it will take proof of intent that the obscenity be *communicated* in some fashion to someone or to a generalized audience.

**Element (2).** The product of dissemination can be either material or a performance. G.S. 14-190.1(a) sets out four broad and overlapping categories that delineate differing modes of dissemination of obscene material and performances. Category (1) is aimed at physical transfers of obscene material. Category (2) refers to live performances. Category (3) is aimed at distributions of material in which there is no clear-cut transfer to a specific person; the term "publishes" probably will be interpreted to refer to publication in the legal sense— that is, *making public* rather than just printing material. Category (4) is aimed at the transmission of obscenity via electronic media. It would cover videotapes, laser discs, television and radio broadcasts, and cable transmissions, as well as motion pictures, still photographs, and audio or audio-visual recordings distributed via radio, TV, telephonic devices, or computer.

Under general principles of law, those who aid and abet the dissemination may be prosecuted for the offense of disseminating obscenity. However, the willing *recipient* or *buyer* is not an aider and abettor; according to a rule of statutory interpretation, when a statute makes only one party in a two-party transaction criminally liable, the other party may not be prosecuted as an aider and abettor.

**"Obscene" defined.** The statute sets out in subsection (b) a definition of "obscene material" that essentially tracks the case law definitions. Because of its case law derivation, this definition would also apply to obscene performances; the word "performance" is then interchangeable with "material." For simplicity, the word "material" will be used in most of this discussion, but most points will apply to performances also.

A number of commentators take the position that the definition of obscenity covers only hard-core pornography—that is, something that goes so far beyond what the community will tolerate that it may be banned totally. Under the statute, material is obscene if *all four* of the following criteria apply:

(1) *"The material depicts or describes in a patently offensive way sexual conduct specifically defined. . . ."* "Sexual conduct" must be specifically defined by statute or case law. Subsection (c) of this statute contains a definition of sexual conduct, which will be separately analyzed below. No matter how offensive the material may be, unless it involves sexual conduct, it is not obscene. Whether the material is patently offensive is a jury question and is to be judged by contemporary community standards (322 N.C. 22; 88 N.C. App. 624). The statute does not specify the geographical limits of the relevant community and a trial judge may permit jurors to apply the standards of their local communities (323 N.C. 159; 322 N.C. 22).

(2) *"The average person applying contemporary community standards relating to the depiction or description of sexual matters would find that the material taken as a whole appeals to the prurient interest in sex."* The jury decides what the contemporary community standards are. As stated above, a trial judge may permit jurors to apply the standards of their local communities (323 N.C. 159; 322 N.C. 159). Jurors will be asked to apply not *their*

standards but the standards of the average person in the community as to sexual matters. The material must be taken as a whole. Many works of art or literature have some pornographic content, but before material may be declared obscene, it is essential that jurors find that as a whole it appeals to the prurient interest in sex. "Prurient" means a morbid or unhealthy interest; cases indicate that some sexually explicit material may only appeal to a healthy curiosity about sex. The statute also specifies "the" prurient interest in sex. This means that a jury could find that the material appeals to the prurient interest in sex of the special audience to which the material is directed, even though it has no such appeal to any juror, as for example the case of material intended specifically for sadomasochists, deviates, or children. Subsection (d) makes this principle explicit.

(3) *"The material lacks serious literary, artistic, political, or scientific value."* The value of material must be decided with reference to the work as a whole (413 U.S. 15; 89 N.C. App. 19; 88 N.C. App. 624). Also, in contrast to the criteria of patent offensiveness and appeal to the prurient interest in sex, the criterion of value must be assessed by reference to the standards of a "reasonable person," not by reference to community standards (481 U.S. 497; 322 N.C. 22; 89 N.C. App. 19; 88 N.C. App. 624; 88 N.C. App. 19; 87 N.C. App. 217). The word "or" means that if the material has serious value of the sort defined by any of the four adjectives, it is not obscene. Some material does deal heavily with prurient themes but nevertheless has serious value. Many commentators, for example, believe that most issues of *Playboy* contain enough of serious literary and artistic interest to forestall a claim that the magazine lacks "serious literary" or "artistic" value—even though a local jury may find that that magazine taken as a whole appeals to the prurient interest in sex. In this case, *Playboy* could not be banned, because subdivision (3) does not apply.

(4) *"The material as used is not protected or privileged under the Constitution of the United States or the Constitution of North Carolina."* This provision is apparently added as a precaution. The other three subdivisions of the statute spell out the currently applicable constitutional standards of obscenity. The phrase "as used" might protect serious researchers who are collecting pornographic material that has no inherent serious value. This is a special case, however, and generally subdivision (4) need not concern judges when they charge juries. Note that such protection has been held to include possession of obscene material in one's own home, although the statute does not expressly address the issue (83 N.C. App. 544, *affirmed*, 320 N.C. 485; 89 N.C. App. 19).

**"Sexual conduct" defined.** Subsection (c) sets out the definition of sexual conduct that the material or performance must depict or describe or embody, listing a variety of acts under three subdivisions. Any act included as an alternative in a subdivision will satisfy the requirement of specificity in the definition of "obscene." This is in contrast to the definition of "obscene" itself, which requires that all four elements of the definition be present. The statute covers:

(1) *"Vaginal, anal, or oral intercourse—whether actual or simulated, normal or perverted."* This means that the material or performance may only simulate intercourse and still meet the definition of sexual conduct.

(2) *"Masturbation, excretory functions, or lewd exhibition of uncovered genitals."* Although "simulated" is not repeated here, the basic statutory definition of obscene material covers material that "depicts or describes" sexual conduct. So if the material *depicts* masturbation, the fact that the actor or model portrayed was only simulating masturbation would be no defense. As to excretory functions, the depiction or description should be in a sexual context—even though the statute does not so specify. In observing this precaution, keep in mind that the sexual context may be deviate or sadomasochistic.

(3) *"An act or condition that depicts torture, physical restraint by being fettered or bound, or flagellation of or by a nude person or a person clad in undergarments or in revealing or bizarre costume."* This subdivision covers sadomasochism that depicts or describes torture, bondage, or flagellation in which either the abuser or the victim is nude, clad in undergarments, or clad in a revealing or bizarre costume. The statute does not specify that the subdivision must be limited to sadomasochism, but this would be wise, for the subdivision is part of a definition of sexual conduct. Sadomasochistic torture, bondage, or flagellation in which the parties are fully and normally clothed is *not* covered by this subdivision. Normally, though, such material will include sexual activity specified in subdivision (1) or (2) as part of the activity and thus will fit into the definition of obscenity.

**Approval of warrant application.** The offense of disseminating obscenity is subject to G.S. 14-190.20, which requires that either a district attorney or an assistant district attorney make the request that a search warrant or criminal process be issued. Criminal process includes the citation, criminal summons, arrest warrant, and order for arrest. The major purpose of this provision is to allow a prosecutor to screen the evidence before a warrant is applied for. The statute does not cover the case of arrests without warrant, and the law is not clear whether arrests without warrant in obscenity cases are valid. No such arrests should be made except in true emergencies.

Note that in 1985 the General Assembly repealed the statutory requirement that material be declared obscene in a civil adversary hearing before a person may be prosecuted for disseminating it. The repeal of that requirement has been upheld as constitutional (83 N.C. App. 544, *affirmed*, 320 N.C. 485; 87 N.C. App. 217), though a defendant has a constitutional nonstatutory right under the First and Fourteenth Amendments to a prompt, post-seizure adversary hearing on the obscenity of seized material pending trial. The burden is on the person seeking return of the material to request a hearing (83 N.C. App. 544, *affirmed*, 320 N.C. 485). Now, the only statutory precondition for prosecution is a prosecutor's request for issuance of criminal process.

**Material contraband.** Subsection (h) provides that obscene material disseminated in violation of G.S. 14-190.1 is contraband. An exception to this statute by case law concerns the possession of obscene material in the *home* for personal use; such material may not be seized. The statute sets out no disposition procedure for contraband obscene material, and therefore a court order should be obtained to dispose of it.

**Only one offense committed during single transaction.** When a person disseminates several obscene items during a single transaction (323 N.C. 439), only one offense is committed.

**Constitutionality.** This section has been upheld as not facially overbroad or vague (83 N.C. App. 544, *affirmed*, 320 N.C. 485).

# CREATING, BUYING, PROCURING, OR POSSESSING OBSCENITY WITH INTENT TO DISTRIBUTE

*Statute*     See G.S. 14-190.1(e) under DISSEMINATING OBSCENITY.

*Elements*    A person is guilty of the offense if that person:
(1) creates *or* buys *or* procures *or* possesses
(2) obscene material
(3) with the purpose and intent of disseminating it unlawfully.

*Punishment*    Class J felony punishable by maximum imprisonment of three years and/or a fine (presumptive sentence one year).

*Notes*    **Element (1).** The alternatives in Element (1) obviously overlap. Buying and procuring are one example. Possession would overlap the other three.

**Element (2).** Refer to the discussion under DISSEMINATING OBSCENITY for a definition of obscene material.

**Element (3).** Before October 1, 1985, only disseminations that occurred in a public place were unlawful. Since that date, *any* dissemination is unlawful. This distinction should be kept in mind in proving the intent to disseminate unlawfully. Refer to the discussion under DISSEMINATING OBSCENITY for a coverage of the broad meaning of "disseminate" with respect to obscene material. There is no crime in simple possession of obscenity, and proof of the intent and purpose required by this element is essential for conviction.

**Approval of warrant application.** G.S. 14-190.20 applies to all offenses in G.S. 14-190.1. Refer to the discussion in the parallel section under DISSEMINATING OBSCENITY.

**Procured material contraband.** Subsection (h) makes obscene material that is "procured" in violation of G.S. 14-190.1 contraband. This would logically cover obscene material that was unlawfully bought as well as material otherwise procured, but it would be safer to have the pleading allege "procure" and to have the jury specify in its verdict the counts on which it is finding a defendant guilty. Such specification will prevent arguments over whether the material is subject to destruction after a conviction. The statute does not state that the obscene material is contraband when the conviction is for *possession* for the purpose of unlawful dissemination. But it may be possible in a hearing to establish that the obscene material had been unlawfully disseminated, procured, or promoted in North Carolina. If so, the judge should be entitled to find the material contraband following a conviction for the possession offense.

---

# ADVERTISING OR PROMOTING SALE OF MATERIAL AS OBSCENE

*Statute*    See G.S. 14-190.1(f) under DISSEMINATING OBSCENITY.

*Elements*    A person is guilty of this offense if that person:
(1) advertises *or* otherwise promotes the sale of
(2) material
(3) that the person represents *or* holds out
(4) as obscene.

*Punishment*  Class J felony punishable by maximum imprisonment of three years and/or a fine (presumptive sentence one year).

*Notes*  **Generally.** This subsection does not require proof that the material advertised or promoted was in fact obscene; it is sufficient if the advertising or promotion represents or holds it out to be obscene. The purpose of this method of drafting is to allow prosecution of promoters even if the obscene material is not found. As a practical matter, though, it may be difficult to secure a conviction under this subsection without introducing the material into evidence. The definition of obscenity requires that the material be judged as a whole and that it lack substantial redeeming value. Most advertisements or promotions will stress the sexual explicitness of the material but may not be detailed enough about the overall character of the material to constitute proof beyond a reasonable doubt that the material is being held out as obscene. The promises of an advertisement or promotion taken in conjunction with the material being hawked put matters into context and help prove the case. If the promotion promises that the material is even more explicit than some other hard-core obscenity, conviction may be possible through introducing into evidence the referred-to material. Even if the material advertised is located and introduced into evidence and is beyond question obscene, the case is not thereby won. A simple advertisement for obscene material that does not imply that the material is obscene fails to fit the elements of this offense. The clear innuendo of the promotion must be that the material is obscene. The advertisement or promotion will rarely explicitly say that the material is "obscene" or that hard-core pornography is the exclusive subject, so proof by innuendo will be the norm in cases under the statute.

**Approval of warrant application.** As noted, G.S. 14-190.20 applies to all offenses in G.S. 14-190.1.

**Promoted material contraband.** Subsection (h) states that obscene material that is "promoted" in violation of G.S. 14-190.1 is contraband. Because a conviction for this offense may be had without proving that the advertised or promoted material was obscene in fact, it will be necessary to establish as a matter of record that the material is obscene before the court may order its destruction.

# PREPARING OBSCENE PHOTOGRAPHS, SLIDES, AND MOTION PICTURES

*Statute*  **§ 14-190.5. Preparation of obscene photographs, slides and motion pictures.**

Every person who knowingly:
(1) Photographs himself or any other person, for purposes of preparing an obscene film, photograph, negative, slide or motion picture for the purpose of dissemination; or
(2) Models, poses, acts, or otherwise assists in the preparation of any obscene film, photograph, negative, slide or motion picture for the purpose of dissemination, shall be guilty of a misdemeanor punishable by imprisonment for up to one year and a fine of up to one thousand dollars ($1,000).

*Elements*    *I. Photographing—G.S. 14-190.5(1)*

A person is guilty of this offense if that person:
(1) knowingly
(2) photographs
(3) oneself or another person
(4) for purposes of preparing an obscene film *or* photograph *or* negative *or* slide *or* motion picture
(5) for the purpose of dissemination.

*II. Assisting the Photographer—G.S. 14-190.5(2)*

A person is guilty of this offense if that person:
(1) knowingly
(2) models *or* poses *or* acts *or* otherwise assists in the preparation of
(3) an obscene film *or* photograph *or* negative *or* slide *or* motion picture
(4) for the purpose of dissemination.

*Punishment*    Misdemeanor punishable by maximum imprisonment of one year and a maximum fine of $1,000.

*Notes*    **Elements I(1) and II(1).** For each offense the structure of the statute puts the word "knowingly" first, and the word arguably modifies all of the succeeding elements. Proof that an act is done "knowingly" beyond reasonable doubt is often difficult, but the statutory wording probably creates no special problems. The cases establish that knowledge of the obscene nature of material may be proved by proof of knowledge of the material's character or content (361 U.S. 147; 322 N.C. 22; 88 N.C. App. 624; 88 N.C. App. 69; 87 N.C. App. 217; 83 N.C. App. 544, *affirmed*, 320 N.C. 485). Nevertheless, whether material is obscene is a mixed issue of fact and law, and the defendant's belief with respect to the material's obscenity is irrelevant. Probably the crucial bit of knowledge to prove in these offenses is knowledge that the material is being made for the purpose of dissemination.

**Elements I(2, 4) and II(3).** This section was drafted before the widespread use of videotape, laser discs, cable television, etc. This raises an issue of the meaning of the verb "photograph" and the term "motion picture." The obvious legislative intent was to cover all forms of material that capture reproductions of still and moving images, and a court would be justified in interpreting this section to effectuate that intent.

**Approval of warrant application.** This section is covered by G.S. 14-190.20, which requires that a *prosecutor* request the issuance of any search warrant or criminal process. Refer to the discussion in the parallel section under DISSEMINATING OBSCENITY.

**No contraband statute applies.** The only criminal statute governing the contraband status of obscenity is in G.S. 14-190.1(h), and it applies to obscene material "disseminated, procured, or promoted in violation of this section. . . ." Thus there is no statute directly applying to this offense that would authorize destruction of the obscene material prepared in violation of this section. After conviction, a judge may have inherent power under the common law to order destruction of the obscene material, but there is no clear North Carolina law on this point. Given the uncertainties, a prosecutor may consider bringing a concurrent civil nuisance proceeding in factually appropriate cases under G.S. Chapter 19, in addition to the criminal charge under this section.

**Comparison with CREATING, BUYING, PROCURING, OR POSSESSING OB-SCENITY WITH INTENT TO DISTRIBUTE.** Compare G.S. 14-190.1(e), discussed above, which would seem to provide for a much broader, totally overlapping offense. Everyone covered by it is in some way creating or assisting in the creation of obscene material. Under general principles of law, a prosecutor may choose either the felony or the misdemeanor charge, or both.

# USING MINOR TO ASSIST IN OBSCENITY OFFENSE

*Statute*

## § 14-190.6. Employing or permitting minor to assist in offense under Article.

Every person 18 years of age or older who intentionally, in any manner, hires, employs, uses or permits any minor under the age of 16 years to do or assist in doing any act or thing constituting an offense under this Article and involving any material, act or thing he knows or reasonably should know to be obscene within the meaning of G.S. 14-190.1, shall be guilty of a Class I felony.

*Elements*

A person is guilty of this offense if that person:
(1) being eighteen years of age or older
(2) intentionally
(3) hires *or* employs *or* uses *or* permits
(4) a minor under the age of sixteen
(5) to do or assist in doing
(6) any act or thing
(7) constituting an offense under Article 26 of G.S. Chapter 14
(8) involving any obscene material, or act, or thing
(9) that the person knows or reasonably should know
(10) is obscene within the meaning of G.S. 14-190.1.

*Punishment*

Class I felony punishable by maximum imprisonment of five years and/or a fine (presumptive sentence two years).

*Notes*

**Element (2).** The intentional state of mind clearly applies to the act of hiring, employing, using, or permitting. Refer to the discussion of the element "intentionally" under DISSEMINATING OBSCENITY. An important question is whether this element of intent also applies to the defendant's state of mind about the minor's age. See the discussion concerning mistake of age in Element (4) below.

**Element (4).** As noted above, the statute can be interpreted to require that the element "intentionally" apply to the age of the minor involved. If it is so interpreted, no issue of a *defense* based on mistake of age will arise, for the state would have to prove that the defendant both knew and intended to hire, etc., the minor under age sixteen. The more usual interpretation of the statute would restrict the element of intent to the act done rather than to a surrounding circumstance, such as the minor's age. If the courts adopt this approach, the law on mistake of age is germane. This section has never contained a provision relating to mistake of age, and it was not changed in this respect by the 1985 revisions of the obscenity laws. The question of whether a mistake of age would be a defense therefore remains unsettled. The General Assembly in 1985 specified in some of the child-protection sections that mistake of age is no defense, but it is not clear that the legislators focused on the mistake issue in enacting the two 1985 amendments to this section. If mistake of age is a defense, the defendant will have to demonstrate a reasonable and mistaken belief that the minor was not under age sixteen. Indifference to or disregard of the minor's age would be no basis for a defense. In most cases this discussion may be academic, because overlapping offenses that disallow the defense of mistake of age will often be available. See the discussion below on comparison with FIRST-DEGREE SEXUAL EXPLOITATION OF A MINOR.

**Elements (8), (9), and (10).** The statute does not specify that the material, act, or thing must in fact be obscene; it says only that the defendant must have the required knowledge of its obscene character. But the implication is that the material, act, or thing must be obscene and that the state must prove it. In this connection, refer to the discussion above of obscenity under DISSEMINATING OBSCENITY.

**Comparison with FIRST-DEGREE SEXUAL EXPLOITATION OF A MINOR.** Compare G.S. 14-190.16, first-degree sexual exploitation of a minor, which may be charged in almost every instance in which a charge could be brought under this section. That offense is punished more heavily and provides that mistake of age is no defense.

---

# DISSEMINATING OBSCENE MATERIAL TO MINOR UNDER SIXTEEN

*Statute*

**§ 14-190.7. Dissemination to minors under the age of 16 years.**

Every person 18 years of age or older who knowingly disseminates to any minor under the age of 16 years any material which he knows or reasonably should know to be obscene within the meaning of G.S. 14-190.1 shall be guilty of a Class I felony.

*Elements*

A person is guilty of this offense if that person:
(1) being eighteen years of age or older
(2) knowingly
(3) disseminates
(4) to a minor under the age of sixteen years
(5) obscene material
(6) that the person knows or reasonably should know
(7) is obscene within the meaning of G.S. 14-190.1.

*Punishment*

Class I felony punishable by maximum imprisonment of five years and/or a fine (presumptive sentence two years).

*Notes*

**Elements (2) and (3).** The word "knowingly" clearly applies to the dissemination. Refer to the discussion of dissemination under DISSEMINATING OBSCENITY for a parallel discussion, keeping in mind that the standard "knowingly" is a lesser one than "intention-ally." As in the offense above, the important issue is whether the element "knowingly" also applies to the defendant's state of mind with respect to the minor's age. See the discussion below on mistake of age.

**Element (4).** Most of the discussion on mistake of age set out for the previous offense, USING MINOR TO ASSIST IN OBSCENITY OFFENSE, applies here. This section was also amended in 1985, but it may be important to note that the amendments *deleted* a defense for counseling professionals. This deletion could be interpreted as evidence of the General Assembly's intent not to allow defenses to this section, although a defendant could assert that mistake of age is a special application of the common law defense of reasonable mistake of fact—and therefore one that applies unless withheld by the General Assembly.

**Element (5).** The statute literally says "material which he [the defendant] knows or reasonably should know to be obscene. . . ." The fair implication of these words, however, is that the material must be obscene material in fact, and this interpretation is reflected in the listing of elements above. Refer to the discussion under DISSEMINATING OBSCEN-ITY for the definition of obscene material. It should be noted that this section is limited to the dissemination of obscene *material*. The dissemination of an obscene performance to a minor would be charged under G.S. 14-190.1.

# DISSEMINATING OBSCENE MATERIAL TO MINOR UNDER THIRTEEN

*Statute*

**§ 14-190.8. Dissemination to minors under the age of 13 years.**

Every person 18 years of age or older who knowingly disseminates to any minor under the age of 13 years any material which he knows or reasonably should know to be obscene within the meaning of G.S. 14-190.1 shall be punished as a Class H felon.

*Elements*

A person is guilty of this offense if that person:
(1) being eighteen years of age or older
(2) knowingly
(3) disseminates
(4) to a minor under the age of thirteen years
(5) obscene material
(6) that the person knows or reasonably should know
(7) is obscene within the meaning of G.S. 14-190.1.

*Punishment*

Class H felony punishable by maximum imprisonment of ten years and/or a fine (presumptive sentence three years).

*Notes*

**Parallel to DISSEMINATING OBSCENE MATERIAL TO MINOR UNDER SIX-TEEN.** This offense is identical to the one above except that it covers a younger victim and carries a higher penalty. G.S. 14-190.8 was also amended in 1985 to raise the penalty and to delete the exception for counseling professionals.

# DISPLAYING MATERIAL HARMFUL TO MINORS

*Statute*

## § 14-190.13. Definitions for certain offenses concerning minors.

The following definitions apply to G.S. 14-190.14, displaying material harmful to minors; G.S. 14-190.15, disseminating or exhibiting to minors harmful material or performances; G.S. 14-190.16, first degree sexual exploitation of a minor; G.S. 14-190.17, second degree sexual exploitation of a minor; G.S. 14-190.18, promoting prostitution of a minor; and G.S. 14-190.19, participating in prostitution of a minor.

(1) Harmful to Minors.—That quality of any material or performance that depicts sexually explicit nudity or sexual activity and that, taken as a whole, has the following characteristics:

    a. The average adult person applying contemporary community standards would find that the material or performance has a predominant tendency to appeal to a prurient interest of minors in sex; and

    b. The average adult person applying contemporary community standards would find that the depiction of sexually explicit nudity or sexual activity in the material or performance is patently offensive to prevailing standards in the adult community concerning what is suitable for minors; and

    c. The material or performance lacks serious literary, artistic, political, or scientific value for minors.

(2) Material.—Pictures, drawings, video recordings, films or other visual depictions or representations but not material consisting entirely of written words.

(3) Minor.—An individual who is less than 18 years old and is not married or judicially emancipated.

(4) Prostitution.—Engaging or offering to engage in sexual activity with or for another in exchange for anything of value.

(5) Sexual Activity.—Any of the following acts:

    a. Masturbation, whether done alone or with another human or an animal.

    b. Vaginal, anal, or oral intercourse, whether done with another human or with an animal.

    c. Touching, in an act of apparent sexual stimulation or sexual abuse, of the clothed or unclothed genitals, pubic area, or buttocks of another person or the clothed or unclothed breasts of a human female.

    d. An act or condition that depicts torture, physical restraint by being fettered or bound, or flagellation of or by a person clad in undergarments or in revealing or bizarre costume.

    e. Excretory functions.

    f. The insertion of any part of a person's body, other than the male sexual organ, or of any object into another person's anus or vagina, except when done as part of a recognized medical procedure.

(6) Sexually Explicit Nudity.—The showing of:

    a. Uncovered, or less than opaquely covered, human genitals, pubic area, or buttocks, or the nipple or any portion of the areola of the human female breast; or

    b. Covered human male genitals in a discernibly turgid state.

## § 14-190.14. Displaying material harmful to minors.

(a) Offense.—A person commits the offense of displaying material that is harmful to minors if, having custody, control, or supervision of a commercial establishment and knowing the character or content of the material, he displays material that is harmful to minors at that establishment so that it is open to view by minors as part of the invited general public. Material is not considered displayed under this section if the material is placed behind "blinder racks" that cover the lower two thirds of the material, is wrapped, is placed behind the counter, or is otherwise covered or located so that the portion that is harmful to minors is not open to the view of minors.

(b) Punishment.—Violation of this section is a misdemeanor and is punishable by imprisonment for up to six months and a fine of at least five hundred dollars ($500.00). Each day's violation of this section is a separate offense.

*Elements*    A person is guilty of this offense if that person:
(1) displays
(2) material
(3) that is harmful to minors
(4) at a commercial establishment
(5) so that it is open to view by minors as part of the invited general public,
(6) having custody, control, or supervision
(7) of the commercial establishment, and
(8) knowing the material's character or content.

*Punishment*    Misdemeanor punishable by maximum imprisonment and a minimum fine of $500. Each day's violation is a separate offense.

*Notes*    **Element (1).** Unlike repealed G.S. 14-190.11, this section does not give any definitional examples of the word "displays." It does provide certain exceptions to display, but for the most part one must turn to the dictionary or to case law defining the word in other statutes. No mental element such as "intentionally" or "knowingly" is set out in this statute, but the inherent meaning of display is inconsistent with any accidental showing or disclosure of the material.

The statute does not address one issue that may frequently arise. Assume that the contents of an adult magazine are unquestionably "harmful to minors," but the fully displayed cover picture—though provocative—does not show either "sexually explicit nudity" or "sexual activity." Does display of the cover constitute an offense? This issue is treated below under the exceptions to the display offense.

**Element (2).** "Material" is defined in G.S. 14-190.13(2) to mean "pictures, drawings, video recordings, films or other visual depictions or representations but not material consisting entirely of written words."

**Element (3).** The term *harmful to minors* is defined in G.S. 14-190.13(1) to mean "that quality of any material or performance that depicts sexually explicit nudity or sexual activity and that, taken as a whole, has the following characteristics: . . . ." The statute then sets out a three-pronged test, (1)a, (1)b, and (1)c, similar to the test established by the United States Supreme Court (413 U.S. 15), except that it is tied to the community standards applicable to minors. Each word in this three-pronged test is important, and the statute must be studied. All three prongs must be satisfied before any material (or performance) can be regulated. The term only applies to "sexually explicit nudity" or "sexual activity." It is essential to understand the special definitions for these phrases.

*Definition of "sexually explicit nudity."* This phrase is defined in G.S. 14-190.13(6)a and (6)b. Subparagraph a, which designates portions of the body revealed, actually covers *mere* nudity rather than sexually explicit nudity, but this potential overbreadth is immaterial because demonstrating any nudity in a material or a performance would be only the first step in determining whether it is "harmful to minors." The material or performance would still have to meet the three-pronged test mentioned above.

*Definition of "sexual activity."* This phrase, defined in G.S. 14-190.13(5), is a crucial one used in several sections in the child-protection provisions of the 1985 amendments governing obscenity and related offenses. As before, satisfying this definition is only the first step in determining whether any material or performance is "harmful to minors"; application of the three-pronged test will probably prevent any constitutional issues of overbreadth from being effectively raised. The prohibition against depictions of persons portrayed as minors in romantic encounters involving apparent sexual touching has been upheld constitutionally as not facially overbroad (83 N.C. App. 544, *affirmed*, 320 N.C. 485).

*Definition of "minor."* G.S. 14-190.13(3) defines a minor as "an individual who is less than eighteen years old and is not married or judicially emancipated."

**Minors as part of the invited general public.** The wording of this element would require proof that the commercial establishment welcomed the general public and made no attempt to exclude minors from the area of establishment in which material harmful to minors was open to view. Mere evidence that a minor viewed the material would be insufficient. The precautions an establishment may have to take may depend on the public that it normally welcomes. A for-profit art gallery that almost never has any minor patrons may need to take few precautions. Commercial establishments that can expect minors as patrons, or accompanying adult patrons, would need to be far more careful. Note that under this section it is no defense that a minor's parent or guardian may have consented or encouraged the display of the material. In fact, that parent or guardian would probably be guilty as an aider and abettor of the offense set out here.

**Exceptions to "display."** To qualify as an exception to the statute, material must be "placed behind 'blinder racks' that cover the lower two-thirds of the material, . . . wrapped, . . . placed behind the counter, or . . . otherwise covered or located so that the portion that is harmful to minors is not open to the view of minors." Given the context of these exceptions, the word "wrapped" should be interpreted to mean covered with an opaque wrapper that hides the portion of the material harmful to minors. These exceptions, with the catch-all authorizing just a covering of the portion of material harmful to minors, probably answer the question asked above under Element (1) concerning the basic meaning of display. There is probably no display in the first place if the cover of a book or magazine contains no material harmful to minors—so long as the *contents* that fall within the definition are not revealed. The statute merely states that material is "not considered" to be displayed if the provisions of the exception sentence quoted above are met. The statute does not say so explicitly, but avoidance of display probably is an affirmative defense to be raised and proved by the defendant (see the discussion of the affirmative defenses in the offense treated below).

**Aiders and abettors; use of related offense.** Any person who is free to act independently and who aids and abets the manager or owner or other person in supervision or control may be charged with this offense under general principles of law. There would be more doubt, though, in prosecuting any employee who is in the establishment at the same time as the supervisor. If the supervisor leaves and the employee then has custody of the establishment, the employee may be prosecuted. An employee who notices a minor browsing through adult material and fails to stop the perusal may be subject to prosecution under G.S. 14-190.15(a), which is discussed below.

# DISSEMINATING HARMFUL MATERIAL TO MINORS

*Statute*

**§ 14-190.15. Disseminating harmful material to minors; exhibiting harmful performances to minors.**

(a) Disseminating Harmful Material.—A person commits the offense of disseminating harmful material to minors if, with or without consideration and knowing the character or content of the material, he:

(1) Sells, furnishes, presents, or distributes to a minor material that is harmful to minors; or

(2) Allows a minor to review or peruse material that is harmful to minors.

(b) Exhibiting Harmful Performance.—A person commits the offense of exhibiting a harmful performance to a minor if, with or without consideration and knowing the character or content of the performance, he allows a minor to view a live performance that is harmful to minors.

(c) Defenses.—Except as provided in subdivision (3), a mistake of age is not a defense to a prosecution under this section. It is an affirmative defense to a prosecution under this section that:

(1) The defendant was a parent or legal guardian of the minor.

(2) The defendant was a school, church, museum, public library, governmental agency, medical clinic, or hospital carrying out its legitimate function; or an employee or agent of such an organization acting in that capacity and carrying out a legitimate duty of his employment.

(3) Before disseminating or exhibiting the harmful material or performance, the defendant requested and received a driver's license, student identification card, or other official governmental or educational identification card or paper indicating that the minor to whom the material or performance was disseminated or exhibited was at least 18 years old, and the defendant reasonably believed the minor was at least 18 years old.

(4) The dissemination was made with the prior consent of a parent or guardian of the recipient.

(d) Punishment.—Violation of this section is a misdemeanor and is punishable by imprisonment for up to two years and a fine.

*Elements*

## I. Furnishing the Material—G.S. 14-190.15(a)(1)

A person is guilty of this offense if that person:

(1) sells *or* furnishes *or* presents *or* distributes

(2) material

(3) that is harmful to minors

(4) to a minor

(5) with knowledge of the material's character or content.

## II. Permitting Browsing—G.S. 14-190.15(a)(2)

A person is guilty of this offense if that person:

(1) allows

(2) a minor

(3) to review or peruse

(4) material

(5) that is harmful to minors

(6) with knowledge of the material's character or content.

*Punishment*    Misdemeanor punishable by maximum imprisonment of two years and a fine.

*Notes*    **Element (1).** Although there is no mental element of "knowledge" specified in the browsing offense, the word "allows" that is used in the statute implies knowledge and control over the situation and a conscious decision to allow the act in question to occur.

**Elements (2), (4), (5).** The important definitions of "material," "harmful to minors," and "minor" are covered under DISPLAYING MATERIAL HARMFUL TO MINORS.

**Offense applies everywhere.** Whereas the display offense under G.S. 14-190.14 is limited to commercial establishments, this offense applies everywhere, and the statute specifically notes that the dissemination is an offense whether done for compensation or not. Thus, a person who shows a neighbor's seventeen-year-old the latest issue of *Playboy* commits an offense under this section.

**Mistake of age no defense except in one instance.** Subsection (c) provides that mistake of age is not a defense to a prosecution except in one situation covered by the affirmative defenses treated below.

**Affirmative defenses.** Subsection (c) sets out four affirmative defenses, but the defendant must raise the affirmative defense, and then must prove it to the satisfaction of the finder of the fact. Subdivision (3) regarding demanding identification papers represents the only defense of mistake of age allowed; note its extremely tight wording. Subdivision (4) requires the *prior* consent of the parent or guardian.

---

# EXHIBITING HARMFUL PERFORMANCES TO MINORS

*Statute*    See G.S. 14-190.15(b) under DISSEMINATING HARMFUL MATERIAL TO MINORS.

*Elements*    A person is guilty of this offense if that person:
(1) allows
(2) a minor
(3) to view
(4) a live performance
(5) that is harmful to minors
(6) with knowledge of the performance's character or content.

*Punishment*    Misdemeanor punishable by maximum imprisonment of two years and a fine.

*Notes*    **Element (1).** Refer to the discussion under this heading in DISSEMINATING HARMFUL MATERIAL TO MINORS.

**Elements (2) and (5).** The important definitions of "harmful to minors" and "minor" are covered under DISPLAYING MATERIAL HARMFUL TO MINORS.

**Private noncommercial performances prohibited.** Like the offense of DISSEMINATING HARMFUL MATERIAL TO MINORS, this offense applies everywhere—to both public and private performances and without regard to whether any charge is made for entry.

**Mistake of age no defense except in one instance.** Refer to the discussion under this heading in DISSEMINATING HARMFUL MATERIAL TO MINORS.

**Affirmative defenses.** The same affirmative defenses set out above apply to this offense. Refer to the discussion under this heading in DISSEMINATING HARMFUL MATERIAL TO MINORS.

---

# FIRST-DEGREE SEXUAL EXPLOITATION OF A MINOR

*Statute*

**§ 14-190.16. First degree sexual exploitation of a minor.**

(a) Offense.—A person commits the offense of first degree sexual exploitation of a minor if, knowing the character or content of the material or performance, he:

(1) Uses, employs, induces, coerces, encourages, or facilitates a minor to engage in or assist others to engage in sexual activity for a live performance or for the purpose of producing material that contains a visual representation depicting this activity; or

(2) Permits a minor under his custody or control to engage in sexual activity for a live performance or for the purpose of producing material that contains a visual representation depicting this activity; or

(3) Transports or finances the transportation of a minor through or across this State with the intent that the minor engage in sexual activity for a live performance or for the purpose of producing material that contains a visual representation depicting this activity; or

(4) Records, photographs, films, develops, or duplicates for sale or pecuniary gain material that contains a visual representation depicting a minor engaged in sexual activity.

(b) Inference.—In a prosecution under this section, the trier of fact may infer that a participant in sexual activity whom material through its title, text, visual representations, or otherwise represents or depicts as a minor is a minor.

(c) Mistake of Age.—Mistake of age is not a defense to a prosecution under this section.

(d) Punishment and Sentencing.—Violation of this section is a Class G felony. Notwithstanding any other provision of law, except a person sentenced as a committed youthful offender, a person convicted under this section shall receive a sentence of at least six years and shall be entitled to credit for good behavior under G.S. 15A-1340.7, except that such credit shall not reduce the time served to less than three years. A person so convicted shall serve a term of not less than three years, excluding gain time granted under G.S. 148-13. The sentencing judge shall not suspend the sentence and shall not place the person sentenced on probation. Sentences imposed pursuant to this section shall run consecutively with and shall commence at the expiration of any other sentence being served by the person sentenced.

*Elements*

## I. Facilitating Production—G.S. 14-190.16(a)(1)

A person is guilty of this offense if that person:

(1) uses *or* employs *or* induces *or* coerces *or* encourages *or* facilitates

(2) a minor

(3) to engage in or to assist others to engage in

(4) sexual activity

(5) for a live performance or for the purpose of producing material that contains a visual representation depicting sexual activity

(6) with knowledge of the character or content

(7) of the performance or material.

## II. Permitting Sexual Activity for Production—G.S. 14-190.16(a)(2)

A person is guilty of this offense if that person:
(1) permits
(2) a minor
(3) under the person's custody or control
(4) to engage in sexual activity
(5) for a live performance or for the purpose of producing material that contains a visual representation depicting sexual activity
(6) with knowledge of the character or content
(7) of the performance or material.

## III. Transporting Minor for Production—G.S. 14-190.16(a)(3)

A person is guilty of this offense if that person:
(1) transports or finances the transportation of
(2) a minor
(3) through North Carolina or across North Carolina
(4) with the intent that the minor engage in sexual activity
(5) for a live performance or for the purpose of producing material that contains a visual representation depicting sexual activity
(6) with knowledge of the character or content
(7) of the performance or material.

## IV. Producing Material Commercially—G.S. 14-190.16(a)(4)

A person is guilty of this offense if that person:
(1) records *or* photographs *or* films *or* develops *or* duplicates
(2) for sale or pecuniary gain
(3) material that contains a visual representation depicting a minor engaged in sexual activity
(4) with knowledge of the material's character or content.

*Punishment*    Class G felony punishable by maximum imprisonment of fifteen years and/or a fine. Although the presumptive sentence for a Class G felony is four and one-half years, the statute provides that a minimum sentence of six years must be imposed for this offense and three years (excluding gain time) must be served before release.

*Notes*    **Purpose of section.** The purpose of this section is to punish severely persons who engage in the production of pornography in which minors are used as actors or models. In every instance under this section the "visual representation" must be tied to the actual exposure of a minor to sexual activity (83 N.C. App. 544, *affirmed*, 320 N.C. 485). The word "material" is defined in G.S. 14-190.13(2) to include drawings and other pictures, but this aspect of the definition must be disregarded unless there is clear proof that a minor's participation in sexual activity was necessary to the creation of the drawing or picture.

**Territorial jurisdiction.** For North Carolina's courts to have jurisdiction, at least one of the elements of the offense must occur within North Carolina. The encouraging, facilitating, permitting, transporting, or financing may well take place here for the purpose of sexual activity by the minor outside the state; the North Carolina courts will have jurisdiction over the offense even though the sexual activity takes place in another jurisdiction that does not punish the particular sexual activity involved. (Indeed, under the first three subdivisions, if the *purpose* is proved, the offense is committed even when the minor never does in fact engage in the sexual activity anywhere.) Of special importance is the offense under subdivision (4), producing material commercially. If material is duplicated in North Carolina, it is apparently immaterial that the minor's sexual activity may have occurred long ago and even in a foreign country. The United States Supreme Court has ruled that a state's interest in stopping the sexual exploitation of its children is so strong that it may act to punish the production and distribution of pornography that was produced through the use of live children without having to worry about proving time of occurrence or place of origin. There may be a defense if the material was produced without any sexual exploitation of the minor. One illustration cited in a case concerned a serious, nonobscene documentary film of sexual initiation rites in Africa where the sexual activity by the minor being filmed was socially encouraged and approved.

**Sexual activity.** The definition of "sexual activity" is provided in G.S. 14-190.13(5); see DISPLAYING HARMFUL MATERIAL TO MINORS. The broad definition may cause constitutional problems, and courts may give certain of its phrases a narrow interpretation. The parts of the definition that cause particular concern are:

*Certain touchings under subparagraph (5)c.* The subparagraph covers touchings, in an act of apparent sexual stimulation, of the clothed buttocks of another person or the clothed breasts of a human female. It has been upheld constitutionally as not being facially overbroad (83 N.C. App. 544, *affirmed*, 320 N.C. 485). One can imagine a serious, nonobscene drama on sexual abuse of children that might portray such a touching of a child actor. Courts may rule that if the production of serious, nonobscene material or performances nevertheless causes the sexual exploitation of a child actor or model, the state may ban the activity. But to ban relatively harmless touchings of the clothed buttocks or breasts of a professional child actor in the course of a drama, when the sexual stimulation depicted is only simulated, may raise serious constitutional problems.

*Certain depictions of torture or physical restraint under subparagraph (5)d.* Subparagraph d is aimed at sadomasochistic torture, bondage, or flagellation in which either the abuser or the victim is "clad in undergarments or in revealing or bizarre costume." The statute, however, does not restrict the subparagraph only to sadomasochism. As a matter of caution, anyone attempting a prosecution under this section should consider using this part of the definition of "sexual activity" only for material and performances in which the sexual or sadomasochistic context is clear.

*Excretory functions under subparagraph (5)e.* Literally, a photograph of a small boy urinating against a playground fence would be sexual activity by a minor, and anyone who dealt commercially with a photograph of the boy would be subject to prosecution under this section. However, this part of the definition of sexual activity should probably be restricted to excretory functions shown in a sexual context or in a setting in which the depiction is clearly intended to stimulate the viewer sexually. Note that if material is designed for the sexual stimulation of a deviate audience, it may come under the definition of "sexual activity" even though it would not stimulate a normal person sexually.

**Application of section to material and performances involving "minors."** Repealed G.S. 14-190.12, which had similar provisions, applied to material and performances involving minors under sixteen years of age. This section, however, applies to material and performances involving all minors as defined in G.S. 14-190.13(3)—anyone under age eighteen who is not married or judicially emancipated.

**Inference that model or actor was a minor.** Subsection (b) of G.S. 14-190.16 states that "the trier of fact may infer that a participant in sexual activity whom material through its title, text, visual representations, or otherwise represents or depicts as a minor is a minor." The constitutionality of this inference has been upheld (83 N.C. App. 544, *affirmed*, 320 N.C. 485).

**Mistake of age no defense.** Subsection (c) states that mistake of age is not a defense to a prosecution under this section.

**Related offenses.** Compare G.S. 14-190.1(e), which makes it a Class J felony to create obscene material with the purpose and intent of disseminating it unlawfully; G.S. 14-190.5(1), which makes it a misdemeanor to photograph oneself or another for the purpose of preparing obscene material intended for dissemination; G.S. 14-190.5(2), which makes it a misdemeanor to model, pose, act, or otherwise assist in the preparation of photographic obscene material for the purpose of dissemination; and G.S. 14-190.6, which makes it a Class I felony to hire, employ, use, or permit a minor under age sixteen to do anything in violation of Article 26 involving any obscene material, act, or thing. It should be noted that this section on first-degree sexual exploitation does not, in specific terms, cover the person who photographs the minor engaged in sexual activity; but it is difficult to conceive of a situation in which the photographer of child pornography would not be guilty under subdivision (1) of using, employing, inducing, etc., the minor to engage in sexual activity for the purpose of producing the material. In this connection, note that the offense under subdivision (4) is that of photographing the material for sale or pecuniary gain. Compare subdivision (4) with G.S. 14-190.17(a)(1), below, which is identical except for omission of the element "for sale or pecuniary gain."

# SECOND-DEGREE SEXUAL EXPLOITATION OF A MINOR

*Statute*

## § 14-190.17. Second degree sexual exploitation of a minor.

(a) Offense.—A person commits the offense of second degree sexual exploitation of a minor if, knowing the character or content of the material, he:
  (1) Records, photographs, films, develops, or duplicates material that contains a visual representation of a minor engaged in sexual activity; or
  (2) Distributes, transports, exhibits, receives, sells, purchases, exchanges, or solicits material that contains a visual representation of a minor engaged in sexual activity.

(b) Inference.—In a prosecution under this section, the trier of fact may infer that a participant in sexual activity whom material through its title, text, visual representations or otherwise represents or depicts as a minor is a minor.

(c) Mistake of Age.—Mistake of age is not a defense to a prosecution under this section.

(d) Punishment and Sentencing.—Violation of this section is a Class H felony. Notwithstanding any other provision of law, except a person sentenced as a committed youthful offender, a person convicted under this section shall receive a sentence of at least four years and shall be entitled to credit for good behavior under G.S. 15A-1340.7, except that such credit shall not reduce the time served to less than two years. A person so convicted shall serve a term of not less than two years, excluding gain time granted under G.S. 148-13. The sentencing judge may not suspend the sentence and may not place the person sentenced on probation. Sentences imposed pursuant to this section shall run consecutively with and shall commence at the expiration of any other sentence being served by the person  sentenced.

*Elements*

## I. Producing Material Noncommercially—G.S. 14-190.17(a)(1)

A person is guilty of this offense if that person:

(1) records *or* photographs *or* films *or* develops *or* duplicates

(2) material that contains a visual representation of a minor engaged in sexual activity

(3) with knowledge of the material's character or content.

## II. Circulating Material—G.S. 14-190.17(a)(2)

A person is guilty of this offense if that person:

(1) distributes *or* transports *or* exhibits *or* receives *or* sells *or* purchases *or* exchanges *or* solicits

(2) material that contains a visual representation of a minor engaged in sexual activity

(3) with knowledge of the material's character or content.

*Punishment*

Class H felony punishable by maximum imprisonment of ten years and/or a fine. Although the presumptive sentence for a Class H felony is three years, the statute provides that a minimum sentence of four years must be imposed for this offense and that two years (excluding gain time) must be served before release.

*Notes*

**Purpose of section.** Subdivision (1) is aimed at noncommercial production of child pornography; it is identical with G.S. 14-190.16(a)(4), except that the first-degree offense adds the element "for sale or pecuniary gain." Hearings before legislative committees have discussed the cottage industry in which children are sexually exploited by deviates who then swap the material they produce with other deviates. Subdivision (2) is aimed at circulation of the child pornography—whether done commercially or noncommercially. It is intentionally quite broad to allow prosecution of members of the "pedophile network" who sell to or exchange child pornography with each other. It is so broad, however, that it would cover the individual purchase of a nationally circulated magazine that contained a photograph of a model engaging in some indecent but nonobscene "sexual activity," if it turns out that the model was in fact a minor when the photograph was taken. Thus, prosecutions should probably be limited to pedophiles who typically amass large collections of both homemade and commercially produced child pornography.

**Application of section to material produced elsewhere.** Refer to the discussion of territorial jurisdiction under FIRST-DEGREE SEXUAL EXPLOITATION OF A MINOR. The points made there pertain to this offense, and this  section is intended to apply to child pornography without regard to when and where it was produced.

**Broad definition of "sexual activity."** Refer to the discussion of the term "sexual activity" under FIRST-DEGREE SEXUAL EXPLOITATION OF A MINOR. The cautions stated there apply to this offense with even greater force, because this offense covers noncommercial transactions by persons far removed from any personal involvement in sexual exploitation of a minor.

**Inference that model or actor was a minor.** Subsection (b) of this section is a provision on inference as to the age of the apparent minor who participated in sexual activity identical to the one set out in the first-degree offense. The constitutionality of this inference has been upheld (83 N.C. App. 544, *affirmed*, 320 N.C. 485). Refer to the discussion under this heading in FIRST-DEGREE SEXUAL EXPLOITATION OF A MINOR.

**Mistake of age no defense.** Subsection (c) of this section provides that mistake of age is not a defense. This rule may apply more harshly here than in the first-degree offense, because the noncommercial producers and circulators of child pornography will typically have had no dealings with the child involved and may have no basis for knowing the age of the participant in the sexual activity. Whereas commercial dealers and direct participants logically should take the risk of mistake of age, the logic is less strong here. Nevertheless, the General Assembly undoubtedly has the constitutional power to make this rule.

# PROMOTING PROSTITUTION OF A MINOR

*Statute*    **§ 14-190.18. Promoting prostitution of a minor.**

(a) Offense.—A person commits the offense of promoting prostitution of a minor if he knowingly:
   (1) Entices, forces, encourages, or otherwise facilitates a minor to participate in prostitution; or
   (2) Supervises, supports, advises, or protects the prostitution of or by a minor.

(b) Mistake of Age.—Mistake of age is not a defense to a prosecution under this section.

(c) Punishment and Sentencing.—Violation of this section is a Class G felony. Notwithstanding any other provision of law, except a person sentenced as a committed youthful offender, a person convicted under this section shall receive a sentence of at least six years and shall be entitled to credit for good behavior under G.S. 15A-1340.7, except that such credit shall not reduce the time served to less than three years. A person so convicted shall serve a sentence of not less than three years, excluding gain time granted under G.S. 148-13. The sentencing judge may not suspend the sentence and may not place the person sentenced on probation. Sentences imposed pursuant to this section shall run consecutively with and shall commence at the expiration of any other sentence being served by the person sentenced.

*Elements*    *I. Facilitating Minor's Prostitution—G.S. 14-190.18(a)(1)*

A person is guilty of this offense if that person:
(1) knowingly
(2) entices *or* forces *or* encourages *or* otherwise facilitates
(3) a minor
(4) to participate in prostitution.

## II. Protecting Minor's Prostitution—G.S. 14-190.18(a)(2)

A person is guilty of this offense if that person:
(1) knowingly
(2) supervises *or* supports *or* advises *or* protects
(3) the prostitution
(4) of a minor or by a minor.

*Punishment*

Class G felony punishable by maximum imprisonment of fifteen years and/or a fine. Although the presumptive sentence for a Class G felony is four and one-half years, the statute provides that a minimum sentence of six years must be imposed for this offense and three years (excluding gain time) must be served before release.

*Notes*

**Element (1).** This term applies to knowledge of the prostitution activity that the defendant's action is promoting. As will be seen below, the state need not prove that the defendant knew of the prostitute's age.

**Subdivisions overlap.** The differences between the offenses in the two subdivisions are not self-evident. Subdivision (1) (set out in I) may be aimed more at the pimp or other person who directly deals with the prostitute; and subdivision (2) (set out in II) may be aimed more at the organizer of the prostitution business who mainly deals indirectly with the prostitute and whose activities of support and protection are given to persons in the network rather than to the prostitute personally. This may also explain the choice of prepositions in element (4) of the protection offense. The prostitution "of" a minor could refer to the minor's status as a prostitute rather than to specific acts of prostitution; the phrase "prostitution by a minor" would cover the latter situation. The distinctions are not clear-cut and the subdivisions do overlap. Most conceivable offenses of promoting prostitution of a minor could be charged under either subdivision. A person may be guilty of this offense even if the minor does not actually commit an act of prostitution; the mere attempt to corrupt a minor by knowingly promoting such prostitution satisfies the elements of the offense (87 N.C. App. 499).

**Broad definition of "prostitution."** Perhaps the most important thing about this section is the extremely broad definition of "prostitution" set out in G.S. 14-190.13(4) to mean "engaging or offering to engage in sexual activity with or for another in exchange for anything of value." Several points should be made:

(1) The broad definition of "sexual activity" in G.S. 14-190.13(5) means that prostitution of a *minor* will cover many more acts than the sexual intercourse that is the basis for the misdemeanor prostitution offense in G.S. Chapter 14, Article 27.

(2) Sexual activity *for* another is also included in this definition. Thus, a voyeur who pays a minor to masturbate or commit some other act under the broad definition of "sexual activity" would be participating in prostitution. Anyone who facilitates this arrangement could be prosecuted under this section.

(3) Sexual activity performed—or an *agreement* to perform it—in exchange for anything of value constitutes prostitution under this definition. A person who agrees to give a minor a marijuana cigarette in exchange for sexual favors short of intercourse is undoubtedly covered as participating in prostitution, and anyone who facilitates this arrangement can be prosecuted under this section.

**Meaning of word "participate" in subdivision (1).** Subdivision (1) covers facilitating a minor to participate in prostitution. In interpreting this element of the offense, use the dictionary definition of "participate." G.S. 14-190.19 (below) includes this word in its caption, "Participating in prostitution of a minor," but there the word is not used in defining the elements of the offense. Moreover, that offense is aimed exclusively at *customers* of the minor prostitute, whereas the word in this subdivision appears to refer to the *minor's* participation in prostitution.

**Mistake of age no defense.** Subsection (b) provides that mistake of age is not a defense to a prosecution under this section.

# PARTICIPATING IN PROSTITUTION OF A MINOR

*Statute*

**§ 14-190.19. Participating in prostitution of a minor.**

(a) Offense.—A person commits the offense of participating in the prostitution of a minor if he is not a minor and he patronizes a minor prostitute. As used in this section, "patronizing a minor prostitute" means:

(1) Soliciting or requesting a minor to participate in prostitution;

(2) Paying or agreeing to pay a minor, either directly or through the minor's agent, to participate in prostitution; or

(3) Paying a minor, or the minor's agent, for having participated in prostitution, pursuant to a prior agreement.

(b) Mistake of Age.—Mistake of age is not a defense to a prosecution under this section.

(c) Punishment and Sentencing.—Violation of this section is a Class H felony. Notwithstanding any other provision of law, except a person sentenced as a committed youthful offender, a person convicted under this section shall receive a sentence of at least four years and shall be entitled to credit for good behavior under G.S. 15A-1340.7, except that such credit shall not reduce the time served to less than two years. A person so convicted shall serve a term of not less than two years, excluding gain time granted under G.S. 148-13. The sentencing judge may not suspend the sentence and may not place the person sentenced on probation. Sentences imposed pursuant to this section shall run consecutively with and shall commence at the expiration of any other sentence being served by the person sentenced.

*Elements*

*I. Soliciting—G.S. 14-190.19(a)(1)*

A person is guilty of this offense if that person:

(1) solicits *or* requests

(2) a minor

(3) to participate in prostitution

(4) when the person soliciting or requesting is not a minor.

## II. Paying/Agreeing to Pay—G.S. 14-190.19(a)(2)

A person is guilty of this offense if that person:
(1) pays *or* agrees to pay
(2) a minor
(3) to participate in prostitution
(4) when the person who pays or agrees to pay is not a minor.

## III. Paying Afterward under Prior Agreement—G.S. 14-190.19(a)(3)

A person is guilty of this offense if that person:
(1) pays
(2) a minor
(3) for having participated in prostitution
(4) pursuant to a prior agreement
(5) when the person who pays is not a minor.

*Punishment*    Class H felony punishable by a maximum imprisonment of ten years and/or a fine. Although the presumptive sentence for a Class H felony is three years, the statute provides that a minimum sentence of four years must be imposed and that two years (excluding gain time) must be served before release.

*Notes*    **Minor not punishable under this section.** This section is aimed at adults who patronize minor prostitutes. The minor is not subject to prosecution under this section, even though, for example, a seventeen-year-old prostitute may look mature and may have initiated the sexual encounter.

**Subdivisions overlap.** It is obvious that the subdivisions overlap. It is not clear that subdivision (3) (set out in III) covers anything not also covered by subdivision (2) (set out in II).

**Dealing through agent specified in statute.** Subdivisions (2) and (3) specify that paying through the minor's agent or making the agreement to pay with the minor's agent is covered. This is probably unnecessary because general legal principles would cover these indirect dealings. The wording of these subdivisions raises the issue of whether soliciting a minor prostitute through the minor's agent would be covered by subdivision (1). The answer is almost certainly yes.

**Broad definition of "prostitution."** Refer to the discussion under this heading in PROMOTING PROSTITUTION OF A MINOR.

**Mistake of age no defense.** In common with several other of these child-protection offenses, subsection (b) specifies that mistake of age is not a defense to prosecution under this section.

**Related offenses.** Compare the misdemeanor offense of PROSTITUTION AND ASSIGNATION under G.S. 14-204(7) (see page 288 of the book), which applies to sexual intercourse for hire on the part of both the supplier of the service and the recipient. Compare G.S. 14-202.1, INDECENT LIBERTIES WITH A CHILD (see this supplement and page 91 of the book).

# PERMITTING FACILITY TO CONTAIN MULTIPLE ADULT ESTABLISHMENTS

*Statute*    ## § 14-202.10. Definitions.

As used in this Article:

(1) "Adult bookstore" means a bookstore:

   a. Which receives a majority of its gross income during any calendar month from the sale of publications (including books, magazines, and other periodicals) which are distinguished or characterized by their emphasis on matter depicting, describing, or relating to specified sexual activities or specified anatomical areas, as defined in this section; or

   b. Having as a preponderance of its publications books, magazines, and other periodicals which are distinguished or characterized by their emphasis on matter depicting, describing, or relating to specified sexual activities or specified anatomical areas, as defined in this section.

(2) "Adult establishment" means an adult bookstore, adult motion picture theatre, adult mini motion picture theatre, adult live entertainment business, or massage business as defined in this section.

(3) "Adult live entertainment" means any performance of or involving the actual presence of real people which exhibits specified sexual activities or specified anatomical areas, as defined in this section.

(4) "Adult live entertainment business" means any establishment or business wherein adult live entertainment is shown for observation by patrons.

(5) "Adult motion picture theatre" means an enclosed building or premises used for presenting motion pictures, a preponderance of which are distinguished or characterized by an emphasis on matter depicting, describing, or relating to specified sexual activities or specified anatomical areas, as defined in this section, for observation by patrons therein. "Adult motion picture theatre" does not include any adult mini motion picture theatre as defined in this section.

(6) "Adult mini motion picture theatre" means an enclosed building with viewing booths designed to hold patrons which is used for presenting motion pictures, a preponderance of which are distinguished or characterized by an emphasis on matter depicting, describing or relating to specified sexual activities or specified anatomical

areas as

defined in this section, for observation by patrons therein.

(7) "Massage" means the manipulation of body muscle or tissue by rubbing, stroking, kneading, or tapping, by hand or mechanical device.

(8) "Massage business" means any establishment or business wherein massage is practiced, including establishments commonly known as health clubs, physical culture studios, massage studios, or massage parlors.

(9) "Sexually oriented devices" means without limitation any artificial or simulated specified anatomical area or other device or paraphernalia that is designed principally for specified sexual activities but shall not mean any contraceptive device.

(10) "Specified anatomical areas" means:

   a. Less than completely and opaquely covered: (i) human genitals, pubic region, (ii) buttock, or (iii) female breast below a point immediately above the top of the areola; or

   b. Human male genitals in a discernibly turgid state, even if completely and opaquely covered.

(11) "Specified sexual activities" means:

   a. Human genitals in a state of sexual stimulation or arousal;

   b. Acts of human masturbation, sexual intercourse or sodomy; or

   c. Fondling or other erotic touchings of human genitals, pubic regions, buttocks or female breasts.

## § 14-202.11. Restrictions as to adult establishments.

No person shall permit any building, premises, structure, or other facility that contains any adult establishment to contain any other kind of adult establishment. No person shall permit any building, premises, structure, or other facility in which sexually oriented devices are sold, distributed, exhibited, or contained to contain any adult establishment.

No person shall permit any viewing booth in an adult mini motion picture theatre to be occupied by more than one person at any time.

### § 14-202.12. Violations; penalties.

Any person who violates G.S. 14-202.11 shall be guilty of a misdemeanor and shall be imprisoned for a term not to exceed three months or fined an amount not to exceed three hundred dollars ($300.00), or both, in the discretion of the court. Any person who has been previously convicted of a violation of G.S. 14-202.11, upon conviction for a second or subsequent violation of G.S. 14-202.11, shall be guilty of a misdemeanor and shall be imprisoned for a term not to exceed six months or fined an amount not to exceed five hundred dollars ($500.00), or both, in the discretion of the court.

As used herein, "person" shall include:

(1) The agent in charge of the building, premises, structure or facility; or

(2) The owner of the building, premises, structure or facility when such owner knew or reasonably should have known the nature of the business located therein, and such owner refused to cooperate with the public officials in reasonable measures designed to terminate the proscribed use; provided, however, that if there is an agent in charge, and if the owner did not have actual knowledge, the owner shall not be prosecuted; or

(3) The owner of the business; or

(4) The manager of the business.

*Elements*

A person is guilty of this offense if that person:

(1) (a)  being the agent in charge of any building, premises, structure, or facility, *or*

(b)  being the owner of any building, premises, structure, or facility when:

(i) the owner knew or reasonably shown have known

(ii) the nature of the business located therein

(iii) and the refused to cooperate with public officials in reasonable measures designed to terminate the proscribed use *or*

(c)  being the owner of the business [operating an offending adult establishment] *or*

(d)  being the manager of the business [operating an offending adult establishment],

(2)  permits

(3)  the building, premises, structure, or other facility

(4)  that contains any adult establishment

(5)  to contain any other kind of adult establishment.

*Punishment*

Misdemeanor punishable by maximum imprisonment of three months and/or a maximum fine of $300. A person who previously has been convicted of any offense within G.S. 14-202.11 is guilty of a misdemeanor punishable by maximum imprisonment of six months and/or a maximum fine of $500.

*Notes*

**Element (1).** The penalty provision applicable to this section is G.S. 14-202.12, which states that any "person" who violates G.S. 14-202.11 is criminally punishable as indicated. The second paragraph of G.S. 14-202.12 states, "As used herein, 'person' shall include"—and then sets out four classes: (1) agents in charge of facilities, (2) owners of facilities, (3) owners of businesses, and (4) managers of businesses. The word "herein" strictly means only G.S. 14-202.12; but the word "person" is also used in connection with each offense in G.S. 14-202.11, and the penalty provision is interconnected with that section. The statute is unclear whether the word "includes" signifies merely an illustrative list or sets out a closed list of "persons" who can be responsible for violations. The listing of elements above follows a conservative interpretation by setting out the material characterizing the "person" responsible in Element (1). It may be that the list is only illustrative and that the state need not allege or prove any of the matter in Element (1). (If this is true, the restrictions on when a facility owner may be a "person" should be treated as defenses to be asserted by owners of facilities. Refer to the treatment below of a proviso concerning the facility owner, "Defense for owner of facility.")

**Element (2).** The word "permit" implies that the person who permits the activity has a basic awareness of the facts involved, has some power of control, and makes a conscious determination to permit it. Given this, it is not important that, in regard to owners of facilities, the statute sets out detailed provisions about that owner's knowledge and says nothing about the state of knowledge of the other people specified.

**Element (3).** For convenience, in the following discussion the term "facility" will be used instead of the phrase "building, premises, structure, or other facility."

**Element (4).** G.S. 14-202.10(2) lists five kinds of adult establishments:

(1) Adult bookstore;
(2) Adult motion picture theater;
(3) Adult mini-motion picture theater;
(4) Adult live entertainment business;
(5) Massage business.

G.S. 14-202.10 sets out detailed definitions for each of these kinds of adult establishments. These definitions must be studied in detail in the process of investigating and proving a case, but they will not be repeated here.

**Element (5).** The wording of the statute indicates that a facility that *contains* an adult establishment is not permitted to contain any other kind of adult establishment. This apparently means that the first adult establishment has priority over other kinds that may be located in the facility later. It does not limit the number of adult establishments of the *same* kind in any facility, however. The idea of priority is reflected in the wording of Element (1), in which bracketed matter is added to define the owners and managers of businesses who can be prosecuted as responsible parties. The safest interpretation is to prosecute owners and managers of adult establishments if they locate in the same facility *after* another kind of adult establishment is already contained there. Often, of course, a business will run two different kinds of adult establishments as part of the same operation. There is nothing unlawful about this so long as the different kinds of establishments are in different facilities. But when, as is often the case, they are in the same facility, the owner and the manager of the business are both unquestionably liable under this offense.

**Defense for owner of facility.** A proviso to subdivision (2) of the second paragraph of G.S. 14-202.12 states that the owner of the facility may not be prosecuted unless the owner has *actual* knowledge of the violation if there is an agent in charge of the facility. This is in contrast with the knew-or-reasonably-should-have-known standard otherwise applicable to that owner under the wording set out above in Element (1). Note, however, that Element (1) also requires that the facility owner have refused to cooperate with the authorities before the owner can be prosecuted. This would seem to make the proviso redundant in most cases; in the course of refusing to cooperate, the owner would surely have gained the requisite actual knowledge.

**Aiding and abetting.** Any person with independence of action who aids and abets one of the parties named in Element (1) to commit the offense may be prosecuted as an aider and abettor under general principles of law. The naming of these four categories of "persons," however, does raise a question about the liability of employees of a facility or of a business operating an adult establishment that is violating the law. If, as noted above, the listing of persons set out in Element (1) is merely illustrative—so that it is not in fact an element of the crime—a knowing and complicit employee may well be subject to prosecution as an aider and abettor. But if the list is interpreted as a closed list, employees who do not fall within the four categories will probably not be subject to prosecution.

# PERMITTING ADULT ESTABLISHMENT IN FACILITY WHERE SEXUALLY-ORIENTED DEVICES ARE CONTAINED

*Statute*      See G.S. 14-202.11, above.

*Elements*      A person is guilty of this offense if that person:
(1) (a) being the agent in charge of any building, premises, structure, or facility, *or*
   (b) being the owner of any building, premises, structure, or facility when:
      (i) the owner knew or reasonably should have known
      (ii) the nature of the business located therein
      (iii) and the owner refused to cooperate with public officials in reasonable measures designed to terminate the proscribed use *or*
   (c) being the owner of the business [operating an offending adult establishment] *or*
   (d) being the manager of the business [operating an offending adult establishment],
(2) permits
(3) any building, premises, structure, or other facility
(4) in which sexually-oriented devices are sold *or* distributed *or* exhibited *or* contained
(5) to contain any adult establishment.

*Punishment*      Misdemeanor punishable by maximum imprisonment of three months and/or a maximum fine of $300. A person who previously has been convicted of any offense within G.S. 14-202.11 is guilty of a misdemeanor punishable by maximum imprisonment of six months and/or a maximum fine of $500.

*Notes*      **Element (1).** Note the discussion of the concept of priority in PERMITTING FACILITY TO CONTAIN MULTIPLE ADULT ESTABLISHMENTS. The provision here, however, literally appears to say that an adult establishment may not be permitted in any facility in which sexually-oriented devices are sold, distributed, exhibited, or contained. This raises troublesome issues of priority if an establishment that is not an adult establishment begins carrying the devices. An example might be a nightwear shop in a mall in which one adult establishment is already located. There is no clear answer to the question in the statute, and the courts will have to grapple with the issue of priority if a case arises. Also, this provision may raise issues with respect to who the responsible person to charge should be. Could the manager of the nightwear business be charged? The words supplied in brackets in Element (1)(c) and (d) limit the term "business" to businesses that operate adult establishments, but this limitation is not in the statute and may not be appropriate in the situation just given. See the discussion under Element (1) in PERMITTING FACILITY TO CONTAIN MULTIPLE

ADULT ESTABLISHMENTS. In the vast majority of cases it will be an ongoing adult establishment that would wish to maximize its profits by installing a line of sexually-oriented devices, which the statute clearly forbids. The person responsible for operating the adult establishment will have to choose between carrying sexually-oriented devices and operating the adult establishment.

**Element (2).** Refer to the discussion of "permits" under this heading in PERMITTING FACILITY TO CONTAIN MULTIPLE ADULT ESTABLISHMENTS.

**Elements (3), (4).** See G.S. 14-202.10 for the definitions of the various kinds of adult establishments and of "sexually oriented devices." Note that the definition of "sexually oriented devices" was amended in 1985 to exclude contraceptive devices. For convenience, in the following discussion the term "facility" will be used instead of the phrase "building, premises, structure, or other facility."

**Defense for owner of facility.** Refer to the discussion under this heading in PERMITTING FACILITY TO CONTAIN MULTIPLE ADULT ESTABLISHMENTS.

**Aiding and abetting.** Refer to the discussion under this heading in PERMITTING FACILITY TO CONTAIN MULTIPLE ADULT ESTABLISHMENTS.

---

# PERMITTING MULTIPLE OCCUPANCY IN VIEWING BOOTH

*Statute*    See G.S. 14-202.11, above.

*Elements*    A person is guilty of this offense if that person:
(1) (a) being the agent in charge of any building, premises, structure, or facility, *or*
    (b) being the owner of the building, premises, structure, or facility when:
        (i) the owner knew or reasonably should have known
        (ii) the nature of the business located therein
        (iii) and the owner refused to cooperate with public officials in reasonable measures designed to terminate the proscribed use *or*
    (c) being the owner of the business [controlling the viewing booth] *or*
    (d) being the manager of the business [controlling the viewing booth],
(2) permits
(3) any viewing booth
(4) in an adult mini-motion picture theater
(5) to be occupied by more than one person.

*Punishment*    Misdemeanor punishable by maximum imprisonment of three months and/or a maximum fine of $300. A person who previously has been convicted of any offense within G.S. 14-202.11 is guilty of a misdemeanor punishable by maximum imprisonment of six months and/or a maximum fine of $500.

*Notes*    **Element (1).** For convenience, in the following discussion the term "facility" will be used instead of the phrase "building, premises, structure, or other facility."

**Element (2).** Refer to the discussion of the level of awareness and control implied by the word "permits" under Element (2) in PERMITTING FACILITY TO CONTAIN MULTIPLE ADULT ESTABLISHMENTS. The owner or the agent in charge of a facility with multiple stores in it would seldom have the requisite knowledge and power of control over the viewing booths to bring them within the meaning of "permits." Examples could be posed of a continual practice that comes to the attention of the facility owner or manager, but proof of this knowledge would be available only rarely. Of course, the "facility" may be a building owned by a participant in the business of operating a single adult mini-motion picture theater in it; in this instance it may be more feasible to charge the owner, though the wording of the statute as to owners set forth in Element (1) does not fit well.

**Discussions in the two previous offenses generally applicable here.** Because this offense is in the same section as the two previous offenses, is subject to the same definitions, and carries the same penalty, most of the previous points are applicable to this offense also and will not be repeated.

**Particular problem as to employees.** Refer to the discussions of the definition of "person" under Element (1) and the issue of aiding and abetting in PERMITTING FACILITY TO CONTAIN MULTIPLE ADULT ESTABLISHMENTS. The ambiguities cited there cause particular problems with this offense. Suppose that while the manager of an adult mini-motion picture theater is in an office on the premises, an employee sees more than two persons occupying a viewing booth, does nothing about it, and says nothing to the manager. If the listing of persons is a closed list, only the manager may be directly charged. But in this instance the manager does not have the knowledge to do the requisite "permitting"; only the employee has that knowledge. With the other two offenses discussed above, a strong argument can be made for not holding mere employees liable if they have no control over the business operations. To establish that principle, however, may seriously hinder enforcement of this viewing-booth provision.

# 18
# Prostitution

## LOITERING FOR PROSTITUTION

*Notes*    **Constitutionality** [new note to be inserted after **Element (2)**], *p. 292*: The court of appeals has ruled that this statute is not unconstitutionally vague (73 N.C. App. 214).

# 19
# Gambling

## POSSESSION OF SLOT MACHINE

*Notes*

**Element (2),** *p. 301*: Chapter 406 of the Session Laws of 1989 amended G.S. 14-306 to make clear that the exception from the definition of slot machine includes devices manufactured for amusement only, the operation of which depends on the player's "dexterity" (or "skill," which is retained from the former definition). Chapter 406 also applied the definition of slot machine in G.S. 14-306 to various gambling statutes: G.S. 14-296 (slot machine defined); G.S. 14-301 and -302 (operating or possessing slot machine or punchboard); G.S. 14-304 (manufacturing slot machine); and G.S. 14-305 (slot machine agreement made unlawful).

## LEGAL BINGO AND RAFFLES

*Statutes, p. 302*:

[Sections of some of the statutes regulating bingo and raffles were inadvertently omitted from the book; therefore G.S. 14-309.5 through 14-309.15 are reproduced here in their entirety.]

### § 14-309.5. Bingo.

It is lawful for an exempt organization to conduct bingo games in accordance with the provisions of this Part. Any licensed exempt organization who conducts a bingo game in violation of any provision of this Part shall be guilty of a misdemeanor under G.S. 14-292 and shall be punished in accordance with G.S. 14-3. Upon conviction such person shall not conduct a bingo game for a period of one year. It is lawful to participate in a bingo game conducted pursuant to this Part. It shall be a Class H felony for any person: (i) to operate a bingo game without a license; (ii) to operate a bingo game while license is revoked or suspended; (iii) to willfully misuse or misapply any moneys received in connection with any bingo game; or (iv) to contract with or provide consulting services to any licensee. It shall not constitute a violation of any State law to advertise a bingo game conducted in accordance with this Part.

## § 14-309.6. Definitions.

For purposes of this Part, the term:

(1) "Exempt organization" means an organization that has been in continuous existence in the county of operation of the bingo game for at least one year and that is exempt from taxation under section 501(c)(3), 501(c)(4), 501(c)(8), 501(c)(10), 501(c)(19), or 501(d) of the Internal Revenue Code and is exempt under similar provisions of the General Statutes as a bona fide nonprofit charitable, civic, religious, fraternal, patriotic or veterans' organization or as a nonprofit volunteer fire department, or as a nonprofit volunteer rescue squad or a bona fide homeowners' or property owners' association. (If the organization has local branches or chapters, the term "exempt organization" means the local branch or chapter operating the bingo game);

(2) "Bingo game" means a specific game of chance played with individual cards having numbered squares ranging from one to 75, in which prizes are awarded on the basis of designated numbers on such cards conforming to a predetermined pattern of numbers (but shall not include "instant bingo" which is a game of chance played by the selection of one or more prepackaged cards, with winners determined by the appearance of a preselected designation on the card);

(3) Repealed by Session Laws 1983 (Regular Session 1984), c. 1107, s. 5.

(4) "Local law-enforcement agency" means for any bingo game conducted outside the corporate limits of a municipality or inside the corporate limits of a municipality having no municipal police force:

　a. The county police force; or

　b. The county sheriff's office in a county with no county police force;

(5) "Local law-enforcement agency" means the municipal police for any bingo game conducted within the corporate limits of a municipality having a police force;

(6) "Beach bingo games" means bingo games which have prizes of ten dollars ($10.00) or less or merchandise that is not redeemable for cash and that has a value of ten dollars ($10.00) or less; and

(7) "Licensed exempt organization" means an exempt organization which possesses a currently valid license.

## § 14-309.7. Licensing procedure.

(a) An exempt organization may not operate a bingo game at a location without a license. Application for a bingo license shall be made to the Department of Human Resources on a form prescribed by the Department. The Department shall charge an annual application fee of one hundred dollars ($100.00) to defray the cost of issuing bingo licenses and handling bingo audit reports. The fees collected shall be deposited in the General Fund of the State. This license shall expire one year after the granting of the license. This license may be renewed yearly, if the applicant pays the application fee and files an audit with the Department pursuant to G.S. 14-309.11. A copy of the application and license shall be furnished to the local law-enforcement agency in the county or municipality in which the licensee intends to operate before bingo is conducted by the licensee.

(b) Each application and renewal application shall contain the following information:

(1) The name and address of the applicant and if the applicant is a corporation, association or other similar legal entity, the name and home address of each of the officers of the organization as well as the name and address of the directors, or other persons similarly situated, of the organization.

(2) The name and home address of each of the members of the special committee.

(3) A copy of the application for recognition of exemptions and a determination letter from the Internal Revenue Service and the Department of Revenue that indicates that the organization is an exempt organization and stating the section under which that exemption is granted; except that if the organization is a State or local branch, lodge, post, or chapter of a national organization, a copy of the determination letter of the national organization satisfies this requirement.

(4) The location at which the applicant will conduct the bingo games. If the premises are leased, a copy of the lease or rental agreement.

(c) In order for an exempt organization to have a member familiar with the operation of bingo present on the premises at all times when bingo is being played and for this member to be responsible for the receiving, reporting and depositing of all revenues received, the exempt organization may pay one member for conducting a bingo game. Such pay shall be on an hourly basis only for the time bingo is actually being played and shall not exceed one and one-half times the existing minimum wage in North Carolina. The member paid under this provision shall be a member in good standing of the exempt organization for at least one year and shall not be the lessor or an employee or agent of the lessor. No other person may be compensated for conducting a bingo game from funds derived from any activities occurring in, or simultaneously with, the playing of bingo, including funds derived from concessions. An exempt organization shall not contract with any person for the purpose of conducting a bingo game. Except as provided in subsection (e) of this section, an exempt organization may hold a bingo game only in or on property owned (either legally or equitably and the buildings must be of a permanent nature with approved plumbing for bathrooms and not movable or of a temporary nature such as a tent or lean-to) or leased by the organization from the owner or bona fide property management agent (no subleasing is permitted) at a total monthly rental in an amount not to exceed one and one-quarter percent (1¹⁄₄%) of the total assessed ad valorem tax value of the portion of the building actually used for the bingo games and the land value on which the building is located (not to exceed two acres) for all activities conducted therein including the playing of bingo for a period of not less than one year and actually occupied and used by that organization on a regular basis for purposes other than bingo for at least six months before the game; and all equipment used by the exempt organization in conducting the bingo game must be owned by the organization. Unless the exempt organization leases the property in accordance with this subsection, an exempt organization may conduct a bingo game only in or on property that is exempt from property taxes levied under Subchapter II of Chapter 105 of the General Statutes, or that is classified and not subject to any property taxes levied under Subchapter II of Chapter 105 of the General Statutes. It shall be unlawful for any person to operate beach bingo games at a location which is being used by any licensed exempt organization for the purpose of conducting bingo games.

(d) Conduct of a bingo game or raffle under this Part on such property shall not operate to defeat an exemption or classification under Subchapter II of Chapter 105 of the General Statutes.

(e) An exempt organization that wants to conduct only an annual or semiannual bingo game may apply to the Department of Human Resources for a limited occasion permit. The Department of Human Resources may require such information as is reasonable and necessary to determine that the bingo game is conducted in accordance with the provisions of this Part but may not require more information than previously specified in this section for application of a regular license. The application shall be made to the Department on prescribed forms at least 30 days prior to the scheduled date of the bingo game. In lieu of the reporting requirements of G.S. 14-309.11(b) the exempt organization shall file with the licensing agency and local law-enforcement a report on prescribed forms no later than 30 days following the conduct of the bingo game for which the permit was obtained. Such report may require such information as is reasonable and necessary to determine that the bingo game was conducted in accordance with the provisions of this Part but may not require more information than specified in G.S. 14-309.11(b). Any licensed exempt organization may donate or loan its equipment or use of its premises to an exempt organization which has secured a limited occasion permit provided such arrangement is disclosed in the limited occasion permit application and is approved by the Department of Human Resources. Except as stated above, all provisions of this Part shall apply to any exempt organization operating a bingo game under this provision.

## § 14-309.8. Limit on sessions.

The number of sessions of bingo conducted or sponsored by an exempt organization shall be limited to two sessions per week and such sessions must not exceed a period of five hours each per session. No two sessions of bingo shall be held within a 48-hour period of time. No more than two sessions of bingo shall be operated or conducted in any one building, hall or structure during any one calendar week and if two sessions are held, they must be held by the same exempt organization. This section shall not apply to bingo games conducted at a fair or other exhibition conducted pursuant to Article 45 of Chapter 106 of the General Statutes.

### § 14-309.9. Bingo prizes.

(a) The maximum prize in cash or merchandise that may be offered or paid for any one game of bingo is five hundred dollars ($500.00). The maximum aggregate amount of prizes, in cash and/or merchandise, that may be offered or paid at any one session of bingo is one thousand five hundred dollars ($1,500). Provided, however, that if an exempt organization holds only one session of bingo during a calendar week, the maximum aggregate amount of prizes, in cash and/or merchandise, that may be offered or paid at any one session is two thousand five hundred dollars ($2,500).

(b) Repealed by Session Laws 1983 (Regular Session 1984), c. 1107, s. 8.

(c) This section shall not apply to bingo games conducted at a fair or other exhibition conducted pursuant to Article 45 of Chapter 106 of the General Statutes.

### § 14-309.10. Operation of bingo.

The operation of bingo games shall be the direct responsibility of, and controlled by, a special committee selected by the governing body of the exempt organization in the manner provided by the rules of the exempt organization.

### § 14-309.11. Accounting and use of proceeds.

(a) All funds received in connection with a bingo game shall be placed in a separate bank account. No funds may be disbursed from this account except the exempt organization may expend proceeds for prizes, advertising, utilities, and the purchase of supplies and equipment used [in conducting the raffle and] in playing bingo, taxes and license fees related to bingo and the payment of compensation as authorized by G.S. 14-309.7(c) and for the purposes set forth below for the remaining proceeds. Such payments shall be made by consecutively numbered checks. Any proceeds available in the account after payment of the above expenses shall inure to the exempt organization to be used for religious, charitable, civic, scientific, testing, public safety, literary, or educational purposes or for purchasing, constructing, maintaining, operating or using equipment or land or a building or improvements thereto owned by and for the exempt organization and used for civic purposes or made available by the exempt organization for use by the general public from time to time, or to foster amateur sports competition, or for the prevention of cruelty to children or animals, provided that no proceeds shall be used or expended for social functions for the members of the exempt organization.

(b) An audit of the account required by subsection (a) of this section shall be prepared annually for the period of January 1 through December 31 or otherwise as directed by the Department of Human Resources and shall be filed with the Department of Human Resources and the local law-enforcement agency at a time directed by the Department of Human Resources. The audit shall be prepared on a form approved by the Department of Human Resources and shall include the following information:

(1) The number of bingo games conducted or sponsored by the exempt organization;
(2) The location and date at which each bingo game was conducted and the prize awarded;
(3) The gross receipts of each bingo game;
(4) The cost or amount of any prize given at each bingo game;
(5) The amount paid in prizes at each session;
(6) The net return to the exempt organization; and
(7) The disbursements from the separate account and the purpose of those disbursements, including the date of each transaction and the name and address of each payee.

(c) Any person who shall willfully furnish, supply, or otherwise give false information in any audit or statement filed pursuant to this section shall be guilty of a misdemeanor.

(d) All books, papers, records and documents relevant to determining whether an organization has acted or is acting in compliance with this section shall be open to inspection by the law-enforcement agency or its designee, or the district attorney or his designee, or the Department of Human Resources at reasonable times and during reasonable hours.

### § 14-309.12. Violation is gambling.

A bingo game conducted otherwise than in accordance with the provisions of this Part is "gambling" within the meaning of G.S. 19-1 et seq., and proceedings against such bingo game may be instituted as provided for in Chapter 19 of the General Statutes.

### § 14-309.13. Public sessions.

Any exempt organization operating a bingo game which is open to persons other than members of the exempt organization, their spouses, and their children shall make such bingo game open to the general public.

### § 14-309.14. Beach bingo.

Nothing in this Article shall apply to "beach bingo" games except for the following subsections:

(a) No beach bingo game may be held in conjunction with any other lawful bingo game, with any "promotional bingo game", or with any offering of an opportunity to obtain anything of value by chance, whether for valuable consideration or not. Any person who violates this subsection is guilty of a Class H felony.

(b) G.S. 18B-308 shall apply to beach bingo games.

### § 14-309.15. Raffles.

(a) It is lawful for any nonprofit organization or association, recognized by the Department of Revenue as tax-exempt pursuant to G.S. 105-130.11(a), to conduct raffles in accordance with this section. Any person who conducts a raffle in violation of any provision of this section shall be guilty of a misdemeanor under G.S. 14-292 and shall be punished in accordance with G.S. 14-3. Upon conviction that person shall not conduct a raffle for a period of one year. It is lawful to participate in a raffle conducted pursuant to this section. It shall not constitute a violation of State law to advertise a raffle conducted in accordance with this section. A raffle conducted pursuant to this section is not "gambling".

(b) For purposes of this section "raffle" means a game in which the prize is won by random drawing of the name or number of one or more persons purchasing chances.

(c) Raffles shall be limited to two per nonprofit organization per year.

(d) The maximum cash prize that may be offered or paid for any one raffle is one thousand dollars ($1,000) and if merchandise is used as a prize, and it is not redeemable for cash, the maximum fair market value of that prize may be twenty-five thousand dollars ($25,000). No real property may be offered as a prize in a raffle.

(e) Raffles shall not be conducted in conjunction with bingo.

(f) As used in this subsection, "net proceeds of a raffle" means the receipts less the cost of prizes awarded. No less than ninety percent (90%) of the net proceeds of a raffle shall be used by the nonprofit organization or association for charitable, religious, educational, civic, or other nonprofit purposes. None of the net proceeds of the raffle may be used to pay any person to conduct the raffle, or to rent a building where the tickets are received or sold or the drawing is conducted.

*Notes* **Bingo,** *p. 305*: Chapter 701 of the Session Laws of 1987 amended G.S. 14-309.14 concerning "beach bingo," *i.e.*, bingo games with maximum prizes of $10.00 or merchandise with a maximum value of $10.00 that is not redeemable for cash. The act prohibited holding a beach bingo game in conjunction with any other lawful bingo game, with any promotional bingo game, or with any offering of a chance to gamble. Violation of these prohibitions is a Class H felony, punishable by maximum imprisonment of ten years and/or a fine (presumptive sentence three years). Chapter 2169 of the Session Laws of 1987 (Regular

Session 1988) transferred responsibility for issuing and renewing bingo licenses from the Department of Revenue to the Department of Human Resources.

A scheme in which a person purchases a comb for $5.00 (when its retail value is nineteen cents) or candy for $1.00 (when its retail value is one cent) and then is given "free" bingo game cards with substantial prizes for winners constitutes bingo (95 N.C. App. 258).

**Constitutionality,** *p. 306*: The court of appeals has ruled that the licensing criteria under G.S. 14-309.7(c) for bingo games that limit rent, prohibit subleasing, and prohibit contracting with bingo operators are constitutional, since they are rationally related to the legitimate goal of ensuring that the money earned by an exempt organization is used for a charitable purpose (79 N.C. App. 156). Under G.S. 14-309.7(c) the requirements about the minimum term of a lease and other uses of a building used for bingo are constitutional, in that they are rationally related to the legitimate goal of ensuring that an exempt organization has community roots (79 N.C. App. 156). The rules under G.S. 14-309.8 prohibiting more than two games a week in a building and requiring the same organization to conduct the games are rationally related to the legitimate goal of ensuring that bingo games are not operated by full-time professionals for a profit (79 N.C. App. 156). The provision of G.S. 14-309.8 prohibiting an exempt organization from conducting two bingo sessions within a forty-eight-hour period is not unconstitutionally vague; also, it does not violate equal protection rights, since it is rationally related to the legitimate interest of limiting bingo to a brief, occasional chance for harmless recreation (82 N.C. App. 583).

# 21

# Drug Offenses

## Part I. Controlled Substances

### SCHEDULING OF SUBSTANCES

**Schedule III,** (G.S. 90–91), *p. 320:*
Chapter 1055 of the Session Laws of 1987 (Regular Session, 1988) added a new subsection (k) to G.S. 90-91 to include anabolic steroids as a Schedule III controlled substance.

### MANUFACTURE OF CONTROLLED SUBSTANCE

*Statute, p. 320:*    [Because several changes have been made to G.S. 90-95 since the book was published, the entire statute is reproduced here to replace the statute reproduced on pages 320-23.]

**§ 90-95. Violations; penalties.**
 (a) Except as authorized by this Article, it is unlawful for any person:
  (1)   To manufacture, sell or deliver, or possess with intent to manufacture, sell or deliver, a controlled substance;
  (2)   To create, sell or deliver, or possess with intent to sell or deliver, a counterfeit controlled substance;
  (3)   To possess a controlled substance.
 (b) Except as provided in subsections (h) and (i) of this section, any person who violates G.S. 90-95(a)(1) with respect to:
  (1)   A controlled substance classified in Schedule I or II shall be punished as a Class H felon;
  (2)   A controlled substance classified in Schedule III, IV, V, or VI shall be punished as a Class I felon, but the transfer of less than 5 grams of marijuana for no remuneration shall not constitute a delivery in violation of G.S. 90-95(a)(1).
 (c) Any person who violates G.S. 90-95(a)(2) shall be punished as a Class I felon.

(d) Except as provided in subsections (h) and (i) of this section, any person who violates G.S. 90-95(a)(3) with respect to:

(1)  A controlled substance classified in Schedule I shall be punished as a Class I felon;

(2)  A controlled substance classified in Schedule II, III, or IV shall be guilty of a misdemeanor and shall be sentenced to a term of imprisonment of not more than two years or fined not more than two thousand dollars ($2,000), or both in the discretion of the court. If the controlled substance exceeds four tablets, capsules, or other dosage units or equivalent quantity of hydromorphone or if the quantity of the controlled substance, or combination of the controlled substances, exceeds one hundred tablets, capsules or other dosage units, or equivalent quantity, the violation shall be punishable as a Class I felony. If the controlled substance is phencyclidine, or cocaine and any salt, isomer, salts of isomers, compound, derivative, or preparation thereof, or coca leaves and any salt, isomer, salts of isomers, compound, derivative, or preparation thereof, or coca leaves and any salt, isomer, salts of isomers, compound, derivative, or preparation of coca leaves, or any preparation thereof which is chemically equivalent or identical with any of these substances (except decocanized coca leaves or any extraction of coca leaves which does not contain cocaine or ecgonine), the violation shall be punishable as a Class I felony.

(3)  A controlled substance classified in Schedule V shall be guilty of a misdemeanor and shall be sentenced to a term of imprisonment of not more than six months or fined not more than five hundred dollars ($500.00), or both in the discretion of the court;

(4)  A controlled substance classified in Schedule VI shall be guilty of a misdemeanor and shall be sentenced to a term of imprisonment of not more than 30 days or fined not more than one hundred dollars ($100.00), or both, in the discretion of the court, but any sentence of imprisonment imposed must be suspended and the judge may not require at the time of sentencing that the defendant serve a period of imprisonment as a special condition of probation. If the quantity of the controlled substance exceeds one-half of an ounce (avoirdupois) of marijuana or one-twentieth of an ounce (avoirdupois) of the extracted resin of marijuana, commonly known as hashish, the violation shall be punishable as a general misdemeanor. If the quantity of the controlled substance exceeds one and one-half ounces (avoirdupois) of marijuana or three-twentieths of an ounce (avoirdupois) of the extracted resin of marijuana, commonly known as hashish, or if the controlled substance consists of any quantity of synthetic tetrahydrocannabinols or tetrahydrocannabinols isolated from the resin of marijuana, the violation shall be punishable as a Class I felony.

(e) The prescribed punishment and degree of any offense under this Article shall be subject to the following conditions, but the punishment for an offense may be increased only by the maximum authorized under any one of the applicable conditions:

(1), (2) Repealed by Session Laws 1979, c. 760, s. 5.

(3)  If any person commits an offense under this Article for which the prescribed punishment includes imprisonment for not more than two years, and if he has previously been convicted for one or more offenses under any law of North Carolina or any law of the United States or any other state, which offenses are punishable under any provision of this Article, he shall be punished as a Class I felon;

(4)  If any person commits an offense under this Article for which the prescribed punishment includes imprisonment for not more than six months, and if he has previously been convicted for one or more offenses under any law of North Carolina or any law of the United States or any other state, which offenses are punishable under any provision of this Article, he shall be guilty of a misdemeanor and shall be sentenced to a term of imprisonment of not more than two years or fined not more than two thousand dollars ($2,000), or both in the discretion of the court;

(5)  Any person 18 years of age or over who violates G.S. 90-95(a)(1) by selling or delivering a controlled substance to a person under 16 years of age shall be punished as a Class E felon;

(6)   For the purpose of increasing punishment, previous convictions for offenses shall be counted by the number of separate trials at which final convictions were obtained and not by the number of charges at a single trial;

(7)   If any person commits an offense under this Article for which the prescribed punishment requires that any sentence of imprisonment be suspended, and if he has previously been convicted for one or more offenses under any law of North Carolina or any law of the United States or any other state, which offenses are punishable under any provision of this Article, he shall be guilty of a misdemeanor and shall be sentenced to a term of imprisonment of not more than six months or fined not more than five hundred dollars ($500.00), or both in the discretion of the court.

(f) Any person convicted of an offense or offenses under this Article who is sentenced to an active term of imprisonment that is less than the maximum active term that could have been imposed may, in addition, be sentenced to a term of special probation. Except as indicated in this subsection, the administration of special probation shall be the same as probation. The conditions of special probation shall be fixed in the same manner as probation, and the conditions may include requirements for rehabilitation treatment. Special probation shall follow the active sentence but shall not preclude parole. If parole is granted, special probation shall become effective in place of parole. No term of special probation shall exceed five years. Special probation may be revoked in the same manner as probation; upon revocation, the original term of imprisonment may be increased by no more than the difference between the active term of imprisonment actually served and the maximum active term that could have been imposed at trial for the offense or offenses for which the person was convicted, and the resulting term of imprisonment need not be diminished by the time spent on special probation. A person whose special probation term has been revoked may be required to serve all or part of the remainder of the new term of imprisonment.

(g) Whenever matter is submitted to the North Carolina State Bureau of Investigation Laboratory, the Charlotte, North Carolina, Police Department Laboratory or to the Toxicology Laboratory, Reynolds Health Center, Winston-Salem for chemical analysis to determine if the matter is or contains a controlled substance, the report of that analysis certified to upon a form approved by the Attorney General by the person performing the analysis shall be admissible without further authentication in all proceedings in the district court division of the General Court of Justice as evidence of the identity, nature, and quantity of the matter analyzed.

(h) Notwithstanding any other provision of law, the following provisions apply except as otherwise provided in this Article.

(1)   Any person who sells, manufactures, delivers, transports, or possesses in excess of 50 pounds (avoirdupois) of marijuana shall be guilty of a felony which felony shall be known as "trafficking in marijuana" and if the quantity of such substance involved:

a.   Is in excess of 50 pounds, but less than 100 pounds, such person shall be punished as a Class H felon and shall be sentenced to a term of at least five years in the State's prison and shall be fined not less than five thousand dollars ($5,000);

b.   Is 100 pounds or more, but less than 2,000 pounds, such person shall be punished as a Class G felon and shall be sentenced to a term of at least seven years in the State's prison and shall be fined not less than twenty-five thousand dollars ($25,000);

c.   Is 2,000 pounds or more, but less than 10,000 pounds, such person shall be punished as a Class F felon and shall be sentenced to a term of at least 14 years in the State's prison and shall be fined not less than fifty thousand dollars ($50,000);

d.   Is 10,000 pounds or more, such person shall be punished as a Class D felon and shall be sentenced to a term of at least 35 years in the State's prison and shall be fined not less than two hundred thousand dollars ($200,000).

(2)   Any person who sells, manufactures, delivers, transports, or possesses 1,000 tablets, capsules or other dosage units, or the equivalent quantity, or more of methaqualone, or any mixture containing such substance, shall be guilty of a felony which felony shall be known as "trafficking in methaqualone" and if the quantity of such substance or mixture involved:

a.  Is 1,000 or more dosage units, or equivalent quantity, but less than 5,000 dosage units, or equivalent quantity, such person shall be punished as a Class G felon and shall be sentenced to a term of at least seven years in the State's prison and shall be fined not less than twenty-five thousand dollars ($25,000);

b.  Is 5,000 or more dosage units, or equivalent quantity, but less than 10,000 dosage units, or equivalent quantity, such person shall be punished as a Class F felon and shall be sentenced to a term of at least 14 years in the State's prison and shall be fined not less than fifty thousand dollars ($50,000);

c.  Is 10,000 or more dosage units, or equivalent quantity, such person shall be punished as a Class D felon and shall be sentenced to a term of at least 35 years in the State's prison and shall be fined not less than two hundred thousand dollars ($200,000).

(3) Any person who sells, manufactures, delivers, transports, or possesses 28 grams or more of cocaine and any salt, isomer, salts of isomers, compound, derivative, or preparation thereof, or any coca leaves and any salt, isomer, salts of isomers, compound, derivative, or preparation of coca leaves, and any salt, isomer, salts of isomers, compound, derivative or preparation thereof which is chemically equivalent or identical with any of these substances (except decocanized coca leaves or any extraction of coca leaves which does not contain cocaine) or any mixture containing such substances, shall be guilty of a felony, which felony shall be known as "trafficking in cocaine" and if the quantity of such substance or mixture involved:

a.  Is 28 grams or more, but less than 200 grams, such person shall be punished as a Class G felon and shall be sentenced to a term of at least seven years in the State's prison and shall be fined not less than fifty thousand dollars ($50,000);

b.  Is 200 grams or more, but less than 400 grams, such person shall be punished as a Class F felon and shall be sentenced to a term of at least 14 years in the State's prison and shall be fined not less than one hundred thousand dollars ($100,000);

c.  Is 400 grams or more, such person shall be punished as a Class D felon and shall be sentenced to a term of at least 35 years in the State's prison and shall be fined at least two hundred fifty thousand dollars ($250,000).

(3a) Any person who sells, manufactures, delivers, transports, or possesses 1,000 tablets, capsules or other dosage units, or the equivalent quantity, or more of amphetamine, its salts, optical isomers, and salts of its optical isomers or any mixture containing such substance, shall be guilty of a felony which felony shall be known as "trafficking in amphetamine" and if the quantity of such substance or mixture involved:

a.  Is 1,000 or more dosage units, or equivalent quantity, but less than 5,000 dosage units, or equivalent quantity, such person shall be punished as a Class G felon and shall be sentenced to a term of at least seven years in the State's prison and shall be fined not less than twenty-five thousand dollars $25,000);

b.  Is 5,000 or more dosage units, or equivalent quantity, but less than 10,000 dosage units, or equivalent quantity, such person shall be punished as a Class F felon and shall be sentenced to a term of at least 14 years in the State's prison and shall be fined not less than fifty thousand dollars $50,000);

c.  Is 10,000 or more dosage units, or equivalent quantity, such person shall be punished as a Class D felon and shall be sentenced to a term of at least 35 years in the State's prison and shall be fined not less than two hundred thousand dollars $200,000);

(3b) Any person who sells, manufactures, delivers, transports, or possesses 28 grams or more of methamphetamine shall be guilty of a felony which felony shall be known as "trafficking in methamphetamine" and if the quantity of such controlled substance or mixture involved:

a.  Is 28 grams or more, but less than 200 grams, such person shall be punished as a Class G felon and shall be sentenced to a term of at least seven years in the State's prison and shall be fined not less than fifty thousand dollars ($50,000);

b.    Is 200 grams or more, but less than 400 grams, such person shall be punished as a Class F felon and shall be sentenced to a term of at least 14 years in the State's prison and shall be fined not less than one hundred thousand dollars ($100,000);

c.    Is 400 grams or more, such person shall be punished as a Class D felon and shall be sentenced to a term of at least 35 years in the State's prison and shall be fined at least two hundred fifty thousand dollars ($ 250,000).

(4)    Any person who sells, manufactures, delivers, transports, or possesses four grams or more of opium or opiate, or any salt, compound, derivative, or preparation of opium or opiate (except apomorphine, nalbuphine, analoxone and naltrexone and their respective salts), including heroin, or any mixture containing such substance, shall be guilty of a felony which felony shall be known as "trafficking in opium or heroin" and if the quantity of such controlled substance or mixture involved:

a.    Is four grams or more, but less than 14 grams, such person shall be punished as a Class F felon and shall be sentenced to a term of at least 14 years in the State's prison and shall be fined not less than fifty thousand dollars ($50,000);

b.    Is 14 grams or more, but less than 28 grams, such person shall be punished as a Class E felon and shall be sentenced to a term of at least 18 years in the State's prison and shall be fined not less than one hundred thousand dollars ($100,000);

c.    Is 28 grams or more, such person shall be punished as a Class C felon and shall be sentenced to a term of at least 45 years in the State's prison and shall be fined not less than five hundred thousand dollars ($500,000).

(4a)    Any person who sells, manufactures, delivers, transports, or possesses 100 tablets, capsules, or other dosage units, or the equivalent quantity, or more, of Lysergic Acid Diethylamide, or any mixture containing such substance, shall be guilty of a felony, which felony shall be known as "trafficking in Lysergic Acid Diethylamide". If the quantity of such substance or mixture involved:

a.    Is 100 or more dosage units, or equivalent quantity, but less than 500 dosage units, or equivalent quantity, such person shall be punished as a Class G felon and shall be sentenced to a term of at least seven years in the State's prison and shall be fined not less than twenty-five thousand dollars ($25,000);

b.    Is 500 or more dosage units, or equivalent quantity, but less than 1,000 dosage units, or equivalent quantity, such person shall be punished as a Class F felon and shall be sentenced to a term of at least 14 years in the State's prison and shall be fined not less than fifty thousand dollars ($50,000);

c.    Is 1,000 or more dosage units, or equivalent quantity, such person shall be punished as a Class D felon and shall be sentenced to a term of at least 35 years in the State's prison and shall be fined not less than two hundred thousand dollars ($200,000).

(5)    Except as provided in this subdivision, a person being sentenced under this subsection may not receive a suspended sentence or be placed on probation. A person sentenced under this subsection as a committed youthful offender shall be eligible for release or parole no earlier than that person would have been had he been sentenced under this subsection as a regular offender. The sentencing judge may reduce the fine, or impose a prison term less than the applicable minimum prison term provided by this subsection, or suspend the prison term imposed and place a person on probation when such person has, to the best of his knowledge, provided substantial assistance in the identification, arrest, or conviction of any accomplices, accessories, co-conspirators, or principals if the sentencing judge enters in the record a finding that the person to be sentenced has rendered such substantial assistance.

(6)    Sentences imposed pursuant to this subsection shall run consecutively with and shall commence at the expiration of any sentence being served by the person sentenced hereunder.

(i) The penalties provided in subsection (h) of this section shall also apply to any person who is convicted of conspiracy to commit any of the offenses described in subsection (h) of this section.

*Notes*    **Element (1),** *p. 324*: North Carolina does not accept the doctrine, accepted in some jurisdictions, that knowledge includes "willful blindness" of a highly probable fact (that is, deliberate avoidance of knowledge) (324 N.C. 190).

# SALE OR DELIVERY OF CONTROLLED SUBSTANCE

*Notes*    **Element (2),** *p. 325*: For discussions of the definitions of "sell" and "deliver," see 313 N.C. 572, 313 N.C. 122. Sale and delivery of a controlled substance are separate offenses; a verdict finding a defendant guilty of "selling or delivering" a controlled substance is fatally ambiguous (313 N.C. 572; 289 N.C. 488).

# POSSESSION OF CONTROLLED SUBSTANCE WITH INTENT TO MANUFACTURE, SELL, OR DELIVER

*Notes*    **Element (4),** *p. 326*: Possession of a controlled substance with intent to sell or deliver is a single offense, since the General Assembly's purpose in prohibiting such possession is to ban possession with intent to transfer, either by sale or delivery. Thus, a verdict finding a defendant guilty of possession of a controlled substance with intent to "sell or deliver" is not fatally ambiguous (313 N.C. 572; 313 N.C. 122). However, possession with intent to manufacture is a separate offense from possession with intent to sell or deliver and should be submitted separately to the jury (78 N.C. App. 68). When a defendant possessed 4.27 grams of cocaine packaged in twenty separate envelopes and also possessed a large amount of cash, there was sufficient evidence of intent to sell the cocaine (91 N.C. App. 707).

# POSSESSION OF CONTROLLED SUBSTANCE

*Punishment, p. 330*:    Chapters 569 and 675 of the Session Laws of 1985 and Chapter 641 of the Session Laws of 1989 made changes in the punishment for cocaine, dilaudid (hydromorphone), phencyclidine, and marijuana and other Schedule VI substances. Delete the discussion of punishment for Schedules II, III, IV, and VI substances and substitute the following (the punishment for Schedules I and V substances have not changed but are provided here for your convenience).] *For a Schedule I substance*, the crime is a Class I felony punishable by maximum imprisonment of five years and/or a fine presumptive sentence two years). *For a Schedule II, III, or IV substance*, if the amount possessed is (a) more than 100 tablets, capsules, or dosage units, or (b) more than four tablets, capsules, dosage units of dilaudid (chemically known as "hydromorphone"), or (c) any amount of cocaine or phencyclidine, the crime is a Class I felony punishable by maximum imprisonment of five years and/or a fine (presumptive sentence two years). For possession of a lesser amount of a Schedule II, III, or IV substance, the crime is a misdemeanor punishable by maximum imprisonment of two years and/or a maximum fine of $2,000. *For a Schedule V substance*, the crime is a misdemeanor punishable by maximum imprisonment of six months and/or a maximum fine of $500. *For a Schedule VI substance*, (a) a defendant's first conviction for possession of up to a half-ounce of marijuana is punishable by maximum imprisonment of thirty days, and/or a maximum fine of $100; a sentence of imprisonment must be suspended and the defendant may not be required to serve active time as a special condition of probation; (b) possession of more than a half-ounce of marijuana and up to one and a half ounces of marijuana or more than one-twentieth of an ounce and up to three-twentieths of an ounce of hashish is a misdemeanor, punishable by maximum imprisonment of two years and/or a fine; (c) possession of more than one and a half ounces of marijuana, more than three-twentieths of an ounce of hashish, or any amount of synthetic tetrahydrocannabinols or tetrahydrocannabinols isolated from marijuana resin is a Class I felony punishable by maximum imprisonment of five years and/or a fine (presumptive sentence two years).

*Notes*    **Element (2),** *p. 330*: Evidence was sufficient to prove a defendant's constructive possession of a marijuana field three hundred yards behind his house because the defendant admitted knowing marijuana was growing there, he was coming from there when officers first saw him, and he was wearing work clothes and sweating heavily (317 N.C. 643). Evidence was insufficient to prove a female defendant's constructive possession of drug paraphernalia found in her house, because officers had seen two adult males enter and leave the house the day it was searched and adult male clothes were found in closets, and therefore the defendant's control over the premises was not exclusive, and because there was no incriminating evidence linking her to the paraphernalia (320 N.C. 143). In another case, evidence was sufficient to prove a defendant's constructive possession of drugs in a mobile home although he did not have exclusive possession of the mobile home and others were present with the defendant when officers found the drugs, because the defendant's name was on a bill of sale for a mobile home that matched this particular home's description, a bottle of prescription drugs with the defendant's name was found on a coffee table beside the chair in which he was sitting when the officers arrived, and white tablets were in his pants pockets (325 N.C. 693). Similarly, evidence was sufficient to prove a female defendant's constructive possession when cocaine was found in the bedroom of a house while the defendant was in the kitchen during the search, evidence showed that she lived there, women's clothes were in the bedroom and in the dresser where the cocaine was found, and letters with the defendant's name on them were also in the bedroom (87 N.C. App. 380). Again, evidence was sufficient to prove a defendant's constructive possession of marijuana and cocaine found in four different rooms in a house, some of it hidden and some in plain view, even though she was not present when the drugs were found, because evidence showed that a telephone bill and other mail addressed to the defendant at the house address were found in the bedroom, the defendant's minor son (who did not live there) appeared at the house during the course of the officers' search, and an acquaintance of the defendant (who did not live there) was in the living room when officers arrived; this defendant was arrested in the house ten days after the search (89 N.C. App. 123). Evidence was sufficient to prove a defendant's constructive possession of cocaine found in a room where the defendant and others were present when the defendant's key fit a padlock on the building's front door and a rent receipt for the premises along with $10,638 were found in his pocket (91 N.C. App. 707). Evidence was sufficient to prove a defendant's constructive possession of cocaine when an officer heard glass breaking on the other side of a closed door and opened the door to find the defendant and another person in the room, the defendant standing near a broken window and three feet from a table which had cocaine and drug paraphernalia on it. A jury could infer that the defendant was either attempting to escape from the house or was preparing to dispose of the cocaine through the broken window (93 N.C. App. 496). Evidence was insufficient to prove a defendant's constructive possession of cocaine found in a building (when he and three others were present) when evidence did not show that he exercised ownership or possession of building; even though there was evidence that he knew cocaine was there, there was not substantial evidence that he had the capability to exercise control and dominion over it (95 N.C. App. 72). However, evidence was sufficient to prove a defendant's constructive possession of cocaine found in a building (when he and three others were present) when evidence showed that the defendant exercised some control by answering the door and telling someone that the business was closed and they were not selling beer, and that the defendant was in the same room where officers found cocaine in plain view, and finally that the defendant had used cocaine in the building (95 N.C. App. 72).

**Testimony concerning identity of drugs,** *p. 331*: The identity of a controlled substance may be proved through the expert testimony of a law enforcement officer; an officer's testimony that the substance was marijuana was sufficient to uphold a conviction (92 N.C. App. 50).

**Lesser-included offenses,** *p. 331*: Possession of a controlled substance is a lesser-included offense of delivery of a controlled substance (71 N.C. App. 55) but not of sale of a controlled substance (283 N.C. 191). Although felonious possession of marijuana is not a lesser-included offense of possession of marijuana with intent to sell and deliver, the charge of felonious possession may be submitted to the jury when the indictment charging possession with intent to sell and deliver alleges the amount possessed if that amount is sufficient for felonious possession (84 N.C. App. 309).

# TRAFFICKING IN MARIJUANA

*Notes*    **Element (2),** *p. 332*: Transport means "any real carrying about or movement from one place to another." A defendant's carrying cocaine from his house to his truck in the driveway and beginning to back out of the driveway is sufficient evidence of transportation (96 N.C. App. 192).

**Element (3),** *p. 333*: Previously, G.S. 90-87(16) defined marijuana for the purpose of the Controlled Substances Act as "the plant Cannabis sativa L." To make it clear that all species of marijuana are included in Schedule VI of the Controlled Substances Act, Chapter 491 of the Session Laws of 1985 redefined marijuana in G.S. 90-87(16) as "the plant of the genus Cannabis."

**Multiple convictions and punishments,** *p. 333*: Trafficking by sale, manufacture, delivery, transportation, and possession are separate offenses for which a defendant may be separately convicted and punished (317 N.C. 545; 316 N.C. 87).

# TRAFFICKING IN METHAQUALONE

*Notes*    **Element (2),** *p. 334*: Transport means "any real carrying about or movement from one place to another." A defendant's carrying cocaine from his house to his truck in the driveway and beginning to back out of the driveway is sufficient evidence of transportation (96 N.C. App. 192).

**Multiple convictions and punishments,** *p. 334*: Trafficking by sale, manufacture, delivery, transportation, and possession are separate offenses for which a defendant may be separately convicted and punished (317 N.C. 545; 316 N.C. 87).

# TRAFFICKING IN COCAINE

*Notes*    **Element (2),** *p. 335*: Transport means "any real carrying about or movement from one place to another." A defendant's carrying cocaine from his house to his truck in the driveway and beginning to back out of the driveway is sufficient evidence of transportation (96 N.C. App. 192).

**Multiple convictions and punishments,** *p. 336*: Trafficking by sale, manufacture, delivery, transportation, and possession are separate offenses for which a defendant may be separately convicted and punished (317 N.C. 545; 316 N.C. 87).

# TRAFFICKING IN OPIUM OR HEROIN

*Notes*    **Element (2),** *p. 336*: Transport means "any real carrying about or movement from one place to another." A defendant's carrying cocaine from his house to his truck in the driveway and beginning to back out of the driveway is sufficient evidence of transportation (96 N.C. App. 192).

**Element (3),** *p. 337*: A heroin mixture that weighed twenty-two grams was sufficient for a trafficking conviction even though the amount of pure heroin in the mixture was less than four grams (94 N.C. App. 710).

**Multiple convictions and punishments,** *p. 337*: Trafficking by sale, manufacture, delivery, transportation, and possession are separate offenses for which a defendant may be separately convicted and punished (317 N.C. 545; 316 N.C. 87).

# TRAFFICKING IN AMPHETAMINE

[This is a new offense added by Chapter 672 of the Session Laws of 1989 to follow **TRAFFICKING IN OPIUM OR HEROIN,** *p. 337*.]

*Statute*   See subdivision (3a) and subsection (i) of G.S. 90-95 under MANUFACTURE OF CONTROLLED SUBSTANCE in this supplement.

*Elements*   A person is guilty of this offense if that person:
(1) knowingly
(2) (a) sells *or* manufactures *or* delivers *or* transports *or* possesses, *or*
    (b) conspires to sell *or* manufacture *or* deliver *or* transport *or* possess
(3) tablets, capsules or other dosage units, or the equivalent quantity, of amphetamine, its salts, optical isomers, and salts of its optical isomers or any mixture containing such substance
(4) to another person (if the person sells or delivers)
(5) and the quantity of amphetamine, its salts, optical isomers, and salts of its optical isomers or any mixture containing such substance is
    (a) 1,000 or more dosage units or the equivalent quantity, but less than 5,000 dosage units or equivalent quantity, *or*
    (b) 5,000 or more dosage units or the equivalent quantity, but less than 10,000 dosage units or equivalent quantity, *or*
    (c) 10,000 or more dosage units or the equivalent quantity.

*Punishment*   *For the amount in (5)(a),* the crime is a Class G felony punishable by a mandatory minimum sentence of seven years (maximum sentence fifteen years) and a mandatory minimum fine of $25,000. *For the amount in (5)(b),* the crime is a Class F felony with a mandatory minimum sentence of fourteen years (maximum sentence twenty years) and a mandatory minimum fine of $50,000. *For the amount in (5)(c),* the crime is a Class D felony with a mandatory minimum sentence of thirty-five years (maximum sentence forty years) and a mandatory minimum fine of $200,000.

    The mandatory minimum sentences for these crimes are considered the presumptive sentences for purposes of the Fair Sentencing Act (92 N.C. App. 494; 77 N.C. App. 425). For drug-trafficking offenses committed on or after July 1, 1981, day-for-day good-time and gain-time credit at statutory rates are required by the Fair Sentencing Act.

*Notes*   **Element (1).** See the note under Element (1) of MANUFACTURE OF CONTROLLED SUBSTANCE on page 324 of the book.

**Element (2).** See the discussion of manufacture, sell, deliver, and possess in the Notes under MANUFACTURE OF CONTROLLED SUBSTANCE on page 324 of the book, SALE OR

DELIVERY OF CONTROLLED SUBSTANCE on pages 324-26 of the book, and POS-SESSION OF CONTROLLED SUBSTANCE on pages 330-31 of the book, as well as in this supplement. See the discussion of conspiracy under CONSPIRACY on pages 24-25 of the book. Transport means "any real carrying about or movement from one place to another." A defendant's carrying cocaine from his house to his truck in the driveway and beginning to back out of the driveway is sufficient evidence of transportation (96 N.C. App. 192).

**Element (3).** This element is satisfied if the tablet, capsule, other dosage unit, or equivalent quantity has any mixture containing amphetamine. The dosage unit need not contain pure amphetamine. Random sampling and testing of tablets is sufficient to establish that all similar-appearing tablets contain amphetamine (see 61 N.C. App. 554, a case involving methaqualone but equally applicable to amphetamine).

**Element (4).** See the note under Element (4) of SALE OR DELIVERY OF CONTROLLED SUBSTANCE on page 325.

**Multiple convictions and punishments.** Trafficking by sale, manufacture, delivery, transportation, and possession are separate offenses for which a defendant may be separately convicted and punished (317 N.C. 545; 316 N.C. 87).

---

# TRAFFICKING IN METHAMPHETAMINE

[This is a new offense added by Chapter 690 of the Session Laws of 1989 to follow **TRAF-FICKING IN OPIUM OR HEROIN,** *p. 337.*]

*Statute*  See subdivision (h)(3b) and subsection (i) of G.S. 90-95 under MANUFACTURE OF CONTROLLED SUBSTANCE in this supplement.

*Elements*  A person is guilty of this offense if that person:
(1) knowingly
(2) (a) sells *or* manufactures *or* delivers *or* transports *or* possesses, *or*
    (b) conspires to sell *or* manufacture *or* deliver *or* transport *or* possess
(3) methamphetamine or any mixture containing such substance
(4) to another person (if the person sells or delivers)
(5) and the quantity of methamphetamine or mixture containing such substance is
    (a) 28 grams or more, but less than 200 grams, *or*
    (b) 200 grams or more, but less than 400 grams, *or*
    (c) 400 grams or more.

*Punishment*  *For the amount in (5)(a),* the crime is a Class G felony punishable by a mandatory minimum sentence of seven years (maximum sentence of fifteen years) and a mandatory minimum fine of $50,000. *For the amount in (5)(b),* the crime is a Class F felony punishable by a mandatory minimum sentence of fourteen years (maximum sentence of twenty years) and a mandatory minimum fine of $100,000. *For the amount in (5)(c),* the crime is a Class D felony punishable by a mandatory minimum sentence of thirty-five years (maximum sentence of forty years) and a mandatory minimum fine of $250,000.

The mandatory minimum sentences for these crimes are considered the presumptive sentences for purposes of the Fair Sentencing Act (92 N.C. App. 494; 77 N.C. App. 425). For drug-trafficking offenses committed on or after July 1, 1981, day-for-day good-time and gain-time credit at statutory rates are required by the Fair Sentencing Act.

*Notes*     **Element (1).** See the note under Element (1) of MANUFACTURE OF CONTROLLED SUBSTANCE on page 324 of the book.

**Element (2).** See the discussion of *manufacture*, *sell*, *deliver*, and *possess* in the Notes under MANUFACTURE OF CONTROLLED SUBSTANCE on page 324 of the book, SALE OR DELIVERY OF CONTROLLED SUBSTANCE on pages 324-26 of the book, and POSSESSION OF CONTROLLED SUBSTANCE on pages 330-31 of the book, as well as in this supplement. See the discussion of conspiracy under CONSPIRACY on pages 24-25 of the book. Transport means "any real carrying about or movement from one place to another." A defendant's carrying cocaine from his house to his truck in the driveway and beginning to back out of the driveway is sufficient evidence of transportation (96 N.C. App. 192).

**Element (3).** The statute prohibits trafficking in methamphetamine or any mixture containing methamphetamine. When a mixture containing methamphetamine is involved, it is the weight of the mixture, not the methamphetamine alone, that determines whether this element is satisfied (see 94 N.C. App. 710, a case involving a heroin mixture that would be equally applicable to a methamphetamine mixture).

**Element (4).** See the note under Element (4) of SALE OR DELIVERY OF CONTROLLED SUBSTANCE on page 325.

**Multiple convictions and punishments.** Trafficking by sale, manufacture, delivery, transportation, and possession are separate offenses for which a defendant may be separately convicted and punished (317 N.C. 545; 316 N.C. 87).

---

# TRAFFICKING IN LSD

[This is a new offense added by Chapter 640 of the Session Laws of 1987 to follow **TRAFFICKING IN OPIUM OR HEROIN,** *p. 337.*]

*Statute*     See subdivision (h)(4a) and subsection (i) of G.S. 90-95 under MANUFACTURE OF CONTROLLED SUBSTANCE in this supplement.

*Elements*     A person is guilty of this offense if that person:
(1) knowingly
(2) (a) sells *or* manufactures *or* delivers *or* transports *or* possesses, *or*
    (b) conspires to sell *or* manufacture *or* deliver *or* transport *or* possess
(3) tablets, capsules, or other dosage units, or the equivalent quantity, of lysergic acid diethylamide, or any mixture containing such substance
(4) to another person (if the person sells or delivers)

(5) and the quantity of lysergic acid diethylamide, or any mixture containing such substance is

(a) 100 or more dosage units or equivalent quantity, but less than 500 dosage units or equivalent quantity *or*

(b) 500 or more dosage units or equivalent quantity, but less than 1,000 dosage units or equivalent quantity *or*

(c) 1,000 or more dosage units or equivalent quantity.

**Punishment**

*For the amount in (5)(a),* the crime is a Class G felony punishable by a mandatory minimum sentence of seven years (maximum sentence of fifteen years) and a mandatory minimum fine of $25,000. *For the amount in (5)(b),* the crime is a Class F felony punishable by a mandatory minimum sentence of fourteen years (maximum sentence of twenty years) and a mandatory minimum fine of $50,000. *For the amount in (5)(c),* the crime is a Class D felony punishable by a mandatory minimum sentence of thirty-five years (maximum sentence of forty years) and a mandatory minimum fine of $200,000.

The mandatory minimum sentences for these crimes are considered the presumptive sentences for purposes of the Fair Sentencing Act (92 N.C. App. 494; 77 N.C. App. 425). For drug-trafficking offenses committed on or after July 1, 1981, day-for-day good-time and gain-time credit at statutory rates are required by the Fair Sentencing Act.

**Notes**

**Element (1).** See the note under Element (1) of MANUFACTURE OF CONTROLLED SUBSTANCE on page 324 of the book.

**Element (2).** See the discussion of *manufacture*, *sell*, *deliver*, and *possess* under MANU-FACTURE OF CONTROLLED SUBSTANCE on page 324 of the book, SALE OR DELIVERY OF CONTROLLED SUBSTANCE on pages 324-26 of the book, and POS-SESSION OF CONTROLLED SUBSTANCE on pages 330-31 of the book, as well as in this supplement. See the discussion of conspiracy under CONSPIRACY on pages 24-25 of the book. Transport means "any real carrying about or movement from one place to another." A defendant's carrying cocaine from his house to his truck in the driveway and beginning to back out of the driveway is sufficient evidence of transportation (96 N.C. App. 192).

**Element (3).** This element is satisfied if the tablet, capsule, other dosage unit, or equivalent quantity has any mixture containing LSD. The dosage unit need not contain pure LSD. Random sampling and testing of tablets is sufficient to establish that all similar-appearing tablets contain LSD (see 61 N.C. App. 554, a case involving methaqualone but equally applicable to LSD).

**Element (4).** See the note under Element (4) of SALE OR DELIVERY OF CONTROLLED SUBSTANCE on page 325.

**Multiple convictions and punishments.** Trafficking by sale, manufacture, delivery, trans-portation, and possession are separate offenses for which a defendant may be separately convicted and punished (317 N.C. 545; 316 N.C. 87).

# OBTAINING CONTROLLED SUBSTANCE BY FRAUD OR FORGERY

*Punishment, p. 342*:    Delete the sentence that sets out the punishment for a misdemeanor violation. By definition the conduct prohibited by this subdivision—a specific intention to deceive—can only be done intentionally; therefore a violation of this provision can only be a felony (78 N.C. App. 239; 73 N.C. App. 645).

# MAINTAINING STORE, DWELLING, OR VEHICLE FOR USE, STORAGE, OR SALE OF CONTROLLED SUBSTANCES

*Punishment, p. 341*:    Unlike OBTAINING CONTROLLED SUBSTANCE BY FRAUD OR FORGERY, discussed above, this crime can be either a felony (when committed "intentionally") or a misdemeanor (when committed "knowingly") (78 N.C. App. 239).

*Notes*    **Element (1),** [new note to be inserted after *Punishment*] *p. 341*: A defendant had sufficient control over a building to be convicted of keeping and maintaining it for the purpose of selling controlled substances when he financed the store there, considered himself married to the woman who controlled the lease, utilities, and liquor license, gave directions to people who were in the store, and was present each time undercover law enforcement officers visited the store (94 N.C. App. 270).

# PUNISHMENT FOR SECOND AND SUBSEQUENT OFFENSES

*Notes*    **Explanation,** *p. 344*: Chapter 675 of the Session Laws of 1985 amended G.S. 90-95(e)(7) to conform to the changes in punishment for possession of marijuana by providing that a defendant convicted of possession of up to a half-ounce of marijuana who previously was convicted of a controlled substances offense is guilty of a misdemeanor punishable by a maximum imprisonment of six months and/or a maximum fine of $500.

# POSSESSION OF DRUG PARAPHERNALIA

*Notes*    **Element (3),** *p. 347*: Triple-beam weighing scales found in a car's trunk in a box next to a suitcase containing cocaine were drug paraphernalia (96 N.C. App. 389).

# FURNISHING CONTROLLED SUBSTANCE TO INMATE

*Notes*     **Exception,** *p. 349*: Chapter 106 of the Session Laws of 1989 amended this statute to permit an ordained minister or rabbi to give sacramental wine to prisoners or jail inmates as part of a religious service.

# 22

# Motor Vehicle Offenses

## IMPAIRED DRIVING

*Notes*

**Element (2),** *p. 360*: Chapter 711 of the Session Laws of 1989 added a new subsection (e) to G.S. 20-138.1 to exclude as a "vehicle" under this offense a bicycle, horse, and lawn mower. (A moped is still a vehicle under this offense.)

**Element (4)(a),** *p. 361*: Even if a defendant's blood alcohol concentration at a relevant time after driving is less than .10, the defendant may still be convicted of impaired driving when a law enforcement officer's testimony includes observations supporting a finding of impairment, such as the quality of the defendant's driving, the odor of alcohol about the defendant's person, and the defendant's poor performance on sobriety tests (74 N.C. App. 479).

**New commercial vehicle impaired driving offense** [new note to be added after **Constitutionality**], *p. 361*: Chapter 771 of the Session Laws of 1989 created a new commercial driver's license system and added a new offense, impaired driving in a commercial vehicle, which becomes effective on September 1, 1990. This offense is committed when a person operates a commercial motor vehicle: (1) while appreciably under the influence of an impairing substance, or (2) after having consumed sufficient alcohol that the person has, at any relevant time after the driving, an alcohol concentration of 0.04 or more. Since this legislation may be amended after this supplement was written and before the law becomes effective, detailed discussion of the new offense will be deferred until the next edition or supplement of this publication.

## HIT AND RUN: FAILURE TO GIVE INFORMATION OR ASSISTANCE WHEN INJURY OR DEATH OCCURS

*Punishment, p. 372*: Chapter 324 of the Session Laws of 1985 changed the punishment for a violation of this misdemeanor offense (as well as for violations of G.S. 20-166(c) and (c1)) to a maximum imprisonment of two years and/or a fine.

# HIT AND RUN: FAILURE TO STOP OR GIVE INFORMATION WHEN INJURY OR DEATH NOT APPARENT OR ONLY PROPERTY DAMAGE OCCURS

*Punishment, p. 373*:    Chapter 324 of the Session Laws of 1985 changed the punishment for a violation of this misdemeanor offense (as well as for violations of G.S. 20-166(b) and (c1)) to a maximum imprisonment of two years and/or a fine.

---

# PASSING A STOPPED SCHOOL BUS

*Statute, p. 377*:    Subsection (f) of G.S. 20-217, which creates a prima facie evidence rule that the registered vehicle owner is the driver of the vehicle that passed the stopped school bus, is no longer in effect, having expired on October 1, 1987.

# Descriptive-Word Index

# Directory of Statutes

Note: Asterisks indicate the statutes reproduced in this supplement.